THE
ESSENTIAL
SELF-COMPASSION
WORKBOOK
FOR
TEENS

THE ESSENTIAL
SELF-COMPASSION
WORKBOOK
FOR
TEENS

OVERCOME YOUR INNER CRITIC
AND FULLY EMBRACE YOURSELF

KATIE KRIMER, MA, LCSW

Illustrations by Yelena Bryksenkova

ROCKRIDGE
PRESS

For general information on our other products and services or to obtain technical support, please contact our Customer Care Department within the United States at (866) 744-2665, or outside the United States at (510) 253-0500.

Rockridge Press publishes its books in a variety of electronic and print formats. Some content that appears in print may not be available in electronic books, and vice versa.

Interior and Cover Designer: Regina Stadnik
Art Producer: Hannah Dickerson
Editor: Lori Tenny
Production Editor: Nora Milman

Illustrations © Yelena Bryksenkova 2020

ISBN: Print 978-1-64611-777-2 | eBook 978-1-64611-778-9

R0

To my teenage self, who could have used some kinder words to get through difficult times. And to you, the reader. May you remember that your pain deserves kindness, always.

Contents

Introduction

I am so excited that you decided to pick up this book! You have taken a brave first step in a journey that will teach you how to be kinder and more compassionate to yourself.

I've been a therapist for seven years, having earned degrees in both psychology and clinical social work. I've worked with many teens just like you, struggling to deal with what is often a difficult, stressful, and overwhelming stage in their lives. It's not unusual for adolescents to feel anxious, depressed, insecure, and lonely. And it's not unusual to respond to these difficult feelings with self-criticism and negative thinking.

Take heart in knowing you are definitely not alone!

It may sometimes seem like there isn't a way out of how bad you are feeling, but the good news is there *is* a path to more relief and joy. It's called self-compassion—a practice that will help you develop a healthier outlook and a more balanced, accepting view of yourself, now and throughout your lifetime.

Self-compassion is a remarkable superpower. In my years of teaching it to teens, I've seen incredibly positive changes in how these young people feel about life in general and themselves

in particular. Those who struggle with perfectionism in school learn to accept and bounce back from their failures. Those who experience rejection learn how to move on, and not get caught up in intense emotions. Teens speak to themselves with warmth and love, and their feelings of confidence and self-worth increase. As they learn how to love and accept themselves, they become less concerned with what their peers think about them.

This workbook will teach you the life-changing magic of self-compassion and transform the way you respond to yourself in tough times. You will learn that your suffering deserves to be met with warmth and acceptance and start treating yourself as if you were your own best friend.

As you go through this workbook, you will first learn about the benefits and core elements of self-compassion. Next, you will learn different skills through a unique set of exercises designed to teach you all the aspects of this beneficial practice. Then, you'll see what self-compassion looks like in real life by reading the stories of several teens who have benefited from the wonders of self-compassion. Finally, you will have the opportunity to put self-compassion into action through a series of journal prompts. Think of journaling as your safe place to always be able to jot down your thoughts and feelings and reframe your perspective.

Don't worry if on some days you don't feel up for practicing the new skills you will learn in this workbook, or if it just feels especially difficult—that's completely normal. Learning a new skill can be challenging, and it takes time. I think it is so cool that you are willing to try! Just know that these skills will only grow and flourish with time, and there will always be moments when you will need them in your life. I hope you're proud of yourself because you are well on your way to becoming a kinder, warmer, more self-compassionate you!

A MOMENT OF SELF-COMPASSION CAN CHANGE YOUR ENTIRE DAY. A STRING
OF SUCH MOMENTS CAN CHANGE THE COURSE OF YOUR LIFE.
—CHRISTOPHER GERMER

CHAPTER 1

Heart of the Matter: The Facts about Self-Compassion

It's time to discover what makes self-compassion so awesome and life-changing. In order for you to become your own best friend and benefit from everything self-compassion has to offer, it's necessary to understand how it positively impacts both your mind and your body.

In this chapter you'll learn this and more, starting with an overview of the ways self-compassion can truly have a positive impact on your life. Then, we'll talk about what self-compassion is and what it is not—correcting the common misunderstanding that it encourages unhelpful behaviors like laziness and self-pity, which is completely untrue!

Once you've become familiar with the amazing superpower of self-compassion, you'll be ready for any obstacles that come your way, making more and more courageous choices to treat yourself with the kindness you've always deserved—especially when you're stressed or struggling.

WHAT'S IN IT FOR ME?

You may wonder how learning to be kind to yourself in difficult situations—especially ones where you feel that you've messed up—could actually be helpful. You may question how you could possibly tame the judging voice in your head that tells you you're not smart enough, good-looking enough, athletic enough, clever enough.

It's there when you fail an exam and name-calls you when you feel embarrassed or rejected. It convinces you that the only way to be motivated, succeed, and be accepted is to listen to its demands and insults.

Like you, most teens have a version of that critical voice taking up an uninvited space in their head and keeping them from finding a different way to respond when experiencing difficulty, discomfort, and pain. Some suffering is inevitable and necessary in life in order to grow, but there's an extra layer of suffering that's brought on by this critical voice—the one that you thought was helping you along but has actually kept you from feeling and being your best.

But guess what? The more you practice self-compassion, the quieter that negative voice becomes until you can't even hear it anymore, making space for more self-confidence, resilience, happiness, and calm. Self-compassion employs a different kind of self-talk that's all about accepting yourself and your struggles as they are, even when things feel like they're going horribly wrong.

This workbook will be your guide to unlearn those self-critical habits and build self-compassionate ones. You can look forward to having a new internal voice that reminds you that you are human, and therefore no matter the struggle or its cause, you deserve acknowledgment, warmth, and relief from your pain.

Let's look at just some of the things practicing self-compassion does to change your life for the better:

Helps you handle difficult situations and painful feelings. When that voice in your head makes a highly self-critical statement—for example, saying you're too ugly to ever get invited or invite someone to the dance—you actually become frightened. Your brain can interpret this fear as a threat, causing you to fight the situation, flee from it, or temporarily shut down. This is known as the "fight-flight-freeze response" or "stress response." When you flee or temporarily shut down, it limits your ability to handle difficult or painful situations in real time. By practicing self-compassion, you can counter the critical voice with a calming statement such as, "I can see that thinking about the dance is so painful for you."

Reduces your stress and anxiety. Calling yourself a failure doesn't inspire a sense of calm—and convincing yourself that you won't pass the upcoming test leads only to worry. But being a supportive friend to yourself will relieve your stress and anxiety, making you feel that you can get through anything and catch yourself if you fall.

Helps you defeat self-criticism. Think of self-compassion as a fearless warrior defending you against self-criticism. Learning to be gentle and accepting toward yourself, your pain, and any shortcomings will eventually wear down and defeat the inner critic altogether.

Builds your emotional resilience. Difficult emotions are part of life. Meeting them with affectionate, nonjudgmental awareness will help you neither get caught up in nor avoid tough feelings. This builds flexibility and makes you more courageous in the face of painful experiences. With self-compassion to comfort you, you know you can weather any storm and bounce back.

Helps you counter faulty core beliefs. Self-compassion helps stop the all-or-nothing nature of negative core beliefs (the strongly held, deep-seated thoughts and assumptions you hold about yourself, others, and the world around you). "I am worthless" becomes "I am human and therefore am worthy." "I am inadequate" becomes "Every teen feels as though they aren't good enough from time to time."

Boosts your feelings of self-worth and your self-image. Acting like your own best friend is the perfect way to conquer shame. Shame tells you that you are "bad" or "not good enough" and makes you believe you are unworthy of belonging and acceptance. Self-compassion allows you to see that you are human (even when you fail) and that there is no precondition for worth. Increasing your feelings of self-worth will make you less likely to care about and be hurt by what others think.

Increases your self-confidence. When your brain assumes that any failure will be met with self-judgment, it attempts to protect you from taking risks in the first place. And it does this by lowering your self-confidence. On the other hand, knowing that you will be compassionate toward yourself even if you fail will give you the courage and confidence to try in the first place. You will feel brave enough to audition for the play, even knowing that you might not make it.

Increases your compassion for others. The more you embrace your imperfect self, the easier it becomes to do that for others. The next time someone is annoying you or acting unkind, you might find yourself being more understanding of their behavior.

Fuels your motivation. Negative self-talk such as, "Don't bother trying. You'll never get it done in time" can be paralyzing. But kinder words such as, "Hey, everyone struggles with procrastination. You have a lot on your plate. You can totally do this!" inspire you to work harder and break the habits that become obstacles to motivation.

Heightens your optimism. A negative perspective on yourself and your experiences makes you feel moody, frustrated, and defeated. Self-compassion changes your perspective. You come to see yourself with more love and acceptance and develop a positive outlook on what is possible for your future—even if the present might be giving you some trouble. Self-compassion gives you the power to eliminate pessimism and see things in a more optimistic light.

Makes you happier. It's simple! Your brain has difficulty creating joy when it's in a state of anxiety, fear, stress, and self-judgment. When you practice self-compassion, your brain's good neurons fire and release positive chemicals into your body, allowing you to stay joyful and present even when there are stressful things going on in your life.

Self-compassion must truly be a superpower if it can do all of that.

I'm excited that you've chosen to learn the skills you'll need to practice self-compassion. But remember that change is not a straight line. There will be times when you hit bumps and curves along the way. Be courageous as you stay on the path. Before you know it, you will have become your own best friend, with an internal strength that will get you through every difficult and uncomfortable experience. I know you can do it!

WHAT IS SELF-COMPASSION, ANYWAY?

To understand what self-compassion is, we first need to define *compassion*. Compassion is the ability to recognize that someone is suffering, express kindness and warmth to that person, and be willing to respond to their struggle in a helpful way. To have compassion for someone means to offer your understanding and kindheartedness when they make mistakes or fail—instead of criticizing or judging them. It also involves acknowledging the person as a fellow human being and accepting their suffering as being a part of the human condition.

Self-compassion is the act of turning that warm-hearted energy inward—toward yourself—especially when you are suffering. The practice involves pausing to acknowledge that something is difficult or that you're hurting and asking how you can comfort and take care of yourself in that moment. We are typically more forgiving and supportive of our loved ones than we are of ourselves. We have a tendency to ignore our own pain or punish ourselves for feeling a certain way. We are also likely to judge and isolate ourselves during difficult times.

Let's break it down a bit more. Dr. Kristin Neff is a psychologist and expert in self-compassion, and she helped develop a program, called Mindful Self-Compassion, specifically for teaching people this awesome skill. She defines self-compassion as having the following three components:

Self-kindness (instead of self-judgment). Being kind to yourself is a simple and powerful alternative to being your own worst critic. The practice involves comforting yourself with words of kindness such as, "This is a difficult emotion to feel" or "It's really tough to fit in." It also involves paying attention to the tone of your inner monologue and noticing if you're being gentle, warm, and loving toward yourself.

Common humanity (instead of isolation). A key component of self-compassion is recognizing that you are not alone. You are part of a common humanity. We are all human, and we all suffer. Every single teen is vulnerable and imperfect. When you blame yourself, you get caught up in a lot of "I" language: "I am never included. I'll never understand this homework. I can't believe how much I procrastinate." Without realizing it, you begin to isolate yourself from everyone else. When you recognize your common humanity, you can comfort yourself in difficult times with thoughts like, "I am not alone in thinking this. I am not alone in feeling this way."

Mindfulness (instead of overidentification). Mindfulness is the practice of paying close attention to what is happening in a given moment, without any judgment. Overidentification is what happens when you start to believe that a thought you are having or an emotion you are feeling is not something you're experiencing but rather who you are. Just because you are experiencing sadness, for instance, doesn't mean being sad is all that's true about your life. It doesn't define you.

As you learn to be mindful of your inner experiences, you will become better at catching yourself in negative thought spirals, noticing how your body feels during a moment of stress, and observing your emotions without suppressing or exaggerating them. You will begin to see how your mind constantly wanders into unhelpful places (as all minds do) and learn to bring your awareness back to the present moment. With a mindful approach, you will come to understand that thoughts are always coming and going, and that they aren't facts.

Self-judgment, isolation, and overidentification are all behaviors that surface when you are struggling. You can learn to overcome them with self-compassion and begin to transform your relationship to your pain. You will develop greater resilience in stressful times, bounce back quicker from difficult days, and embrace yourself when you fail. With self-compassion in your toolkit, you'll start believing in yourself even when you're wary of failure. Your newfound feelings of self-worth will stand up to any criticism because you will know that the safety net of self-acceptance and understanding will always be there to catch you.

WHAT SELF-COMPASSION IS NOT

Self-compassion is often greatly misunderstood. People confuse it with self-pity, self-indulgence, laziness, selfishness, weakness, an excuse for bad behavior—and even self-esteem. None of these could be further from the truth!

Let's take a look at—and correct—these misconceptions:

Self-pity. While self-pity amplifies your problems, self-compassion lets you see a situation with a more mindful perspective and makes it more likely that you'll bounce back more quickly. Imagine that you audition for a play and don't get a part. You feel terrible and refuse to go to school for two days because it feels as though you're the only one who blew the audition. That's self-pity. If you're practicing self-compassion, you will instead try to validate your disappointment by gently telling yourself that not getting a part in a play is just the nature of theater.

Self-indulgence or laziness. One myth about self-compassion is that it will make you less motivated. If you're too comforting to yourself, won't that take away any desire you have to build good habits or get things done? In reality, self-compassion enhances motivation and emphasizes long-term health, not the pleasure of instant gratification. With this practice, you stop shaming yourself into changing and begin motivating yourself with love. It actually makes it less likely that you will engage in harmful self-indulgence out of deep care for your well-being.

Selfishness. You may believe that choosing to be kind to yourself during a difficult time somehow makes you more self-involved. In fact, the less judgmental you are toward yourself, the more resources you have for others. You are not selfish for treating yourself with understanding and love.

Weakness. Self-compassion requires a lot of courage, vulnerability, and strength. There is nothing weak about supporting yourself during a difficult time. Judging yourself or ignoring your suffering will in fact make you weaker by tearing down your feelings of self-worth and lowering your self-confidence.

An excuse for bad behavior. Self-compassion is not a denial of responsibility. In fact, self-compassionate people are more likely to hold themselves accountable for mistakes. Being hard on yourself typically invokes shame, which is an isolating emotion. Shame makes you want to hide because you fear being seen for your mistakes. When you are too fearful to confront what you may have done wrong, you actually end up avoiding responsibility for your mess-up.

Self-esteem. Self-compassion is often confused with its cousin, self-esteem, which is having confidence in your worth or abilities; it's about appreciating and liking yourself. Self-compassion, on the other hand, is about being kind, caring, and accepting to yourself—even, and sometimes especially, at times when your self-esteem might be low.

CONFRONTING YOUR OBSTACLES— WITH CONFIDENCE

The reason I consider self-compassion such a remarkable practice is that it gives people the ability to confidently confront and oftentimes completely overcome the obstacles that are getting in the way of their happiness.

During adolescence, you're faced with so many challenges. You're growing up, but you're not yet an adult, even though sometimes you may like to be treated like one by your parents. Your body is changing, and it may not be changing quickly or "perfectly" enough for your liking. Classes start getting harder, you're meeting new friends but may be growing apart from old ones, and every conversation may seem to circle around the latest crush—or crushing rejection. You may feel the pressure to join clubs, excel academically, get a spot on the sports team, get invited to the dance, babysit your sibling after school—all with the expectation to succeed at everything. You may believe that you must avoid any kind of failure because it makes you bad and unacceptable. You may have a constant feeling that you are "not good enough."

Pressure is likely building on all sides—from your friends, your parents, and your teachers—along with the relentless inner voice that never lets up: "Don't fail the exam." "Don't embarrass yourself." "Make sure you can make people laugh." "Be the smartest one in the room." "You had better be a good kisser." "You have to look your skinniest at the party."

You, like many other teens, may be facing any one or more of the following obstacles:

Anxiety and stress. Adolescence is a time of uncertainty and rapid change. It's made worse by getting yourself stuck in cycles of rumination and worry. Every time you play out a worst-case scenario, your brain activates your nervous system, telling you there's something threatening you. As we covered earlier in the chapter, this is called the fight-flight-freeze response, also known as a stress response. This response fuels feelings of anxiety. Next, you may give yourself a hard time about your perpetual state of worry. It's a vicious cycle that you should do your best to avoid.

Feelings of depression. Your self-esteem takes a hit every time you talk to yourself in an unsupportive way. Chronic low self-esteem can often lead to the development of depressive symptoms. These may include a loss of enjoyment in activities, sadness, mood swings, and feelings of hopelessness and discontent. It's truly a terrible headspace to reside in.

Feelings of insecurity. During adolescence, the list of things that you feel insecure about skyrockets. You may dislike your body, doubt your abilities, fear rejection, worry about disappointing friends or parents, or feel uncomfortable in social settings. The more you judge yourself, the greater the insecurity grows.

Identity confusion. Adolescence is a transition from childhood into young adulthood. You are desperately trying to separate from your parents while still needing their support in many ways. You're navigating all different kinds of relationships (romantic, friendship, etc.) and trying to figure out "who you are."

Feelings of isolation. With a habitual dose of harsh self-judgment and shame, feelings of isolation will start to arise. Those emotions can feel so intense that you may begin pushing others away and spending more time by yourself. Before you know it, you're feeling as though no one could possibly understand what you are going through and that you are entirely alone.

Harmful behaviors. During adolescence, you're trying to figure out ways to cope with the challenges of this stage of life, Some teens turn to harmful coping mechanisms like drug use, self-harm, bullying, or isolation in order to feel "okay."

Being kind to yourself during difficult times probably isn't an option you knew you had, but you certainly do, especially when your inner critic comes knocking on the door. As we discussed in the first part of this chapter, the ways self-compassion can help you improve your life and feel better are vast. With a self-compassionate inner voice, you are better able to tackle any obstacle that comes your way, remembering that you are not alone in your imperfection, being kinder to yourself when you fail, and being accepting and mindful of your emotional experience. Self-compassion will be a flexible coat of armor protecting you from the impact of tough adolescent times, leaving you with more room for joy, calm, and self-exploration.

TIME TO GET STARTED

Now that you know how beneficial self-compassion can be, you're ready to jump into the exercises you will need to strengthen your mindfulness, common humanity, and self-kindness skills. As your inner critic becomes muffled, your vulnerable and worthy self will begin to emerge. Self-compassion will become a guiding light in the darker times of disappointment, hurt, self-doubt, and uncertainty. You will learn how to respond to your mind in a more productive and helpful way, and it will change your relationship to yourself—and to suffering—for the better. I promise that your commitment to the practices across these next pages will be worth it. Get ready to acquire the superpower of self-compassion!

CHAPTER 2

The Basics: Exercises to Build Self-Compassion

It's time to practice, practice, practice! Ahead of you are 50 exercises created to help you gain the awareness and skills of a self-compassionate human. Although it may not seem that every exercise is directly related to self-compassion, rest assured there are many components working together to help you learn how to become more aware of your internal experience. The more aware you are, the sooner you can stop negative thoughts in their tracks and choose instead to focus on your struggle—tending to it with kindness, compassion, and a present state of mind. I suggest you do the first 10 exercises in order, as they set you up for the rest of them. Although several of the quizzes will likely be completed only once, keep in mind that the exercises are meant to be referenced and even repeated as you build your self-compassion skills. Let's do this!

LAYING THE FOUNDATION

HOW SELF-COMPASSIONATE ARE YOU?

This quiz, developed by Dr. Kristin Neff, is a way for you to measure the strength of your self-kindness, common humanity, and mindfulness, which we learned are the key components of self-compassion in chapter 1. I encourage you to complete it at the start and end of the workbook—and at times in-between—to see your progress. To take this quiz online and calculate your self-compassion score, visit Self-Compassion.org/test-how-self-compassionate-you-are.

How I Typically Act Toward Myself in Difficult Times

Please read each statement carefully before answering. To the left of each item, indicate how often you behave in the stated manner, using the following scale:

ALMOST NEVER   1   2   3   4   5   ALMOST ALWAYS

____ 1. I'm disapproving and judgmental about my own flaws and inadequacies.

____ 2. When I'm feeling down, I tend to obsess and fixate on everything that's wrong.

____ 3. When things are going badly for me, I see the difficulties as part of life that everyone goes through.

____ 4. When I think about my inadequacies, it tends to make me feel more separate and cut off from the rest of the world.

____ 5. I try to be loving toward myself when I'm feeling emotional pain.

____ 6. When I fail at something important to me, I become consumed by feelings of inadequacy.

____ 7. When I'm down and out, I remind myself that there are lots of other people in the world feeling like I am.

____ 8. When times are really difficult, I tend to be tough on myself.

____ 9. When something upsets me, I try to keep my emotions in balance.

____ 10. When I feel inadequate in some way, I try to remind myself that feelings of inadequacy are shared by most people.

11. I'm intolerant and impatient toward those aspects of my personality I don't like.

12. When I'm going through a very hard time, I give myself the caring and tenderness I need.

13. When I'm feeling down, I tend to feel like most other people are probably happier than I am.

14. When something painful happens, I try to take a balanced view of the situation.

15. I try to see my failings as part of the human condition.

16. When I see aspects of myself that I don't like, I get down on myself.

17. When I fail at something important to me, I try to keep things in perspective.

18. When I'm really struggling, I tend to feel like other people must be having an easier time of it.

19. I'm kind to myself when I'm experiencing suffering.

20. When something upsets me, I get carried away with my feelings.

21. I can be a bit cold-hearted toward myself when I'm experiencing suffering.

22. When I'm feeling down, I try to approach my feelings with curiosity and openness.

23. I'm tolerant of my own flaws and inadequacies.

24. When something painful happens, I tend to blow the incident out of proportion.

25. When I fail at something that's important to me, I tend to feel alone in my failure.

26. I try to be understanding and patient toward those aspects of my personality I don't like.

CODING KEY:

Self-kindness items:	5, 12, 19, 23, 26	Isolation items:	4, 13, 18, 25
Self-judgment items:	1, 8, 11, 16, 21	Mindfulness items:	9, 14, 17, 22
Common humanity items:	3, 7, 10, 15	Over-identified items:	2, 6, 20, 24

SETTING YOURSELF UP FOR SUCCESS

As with any kind of growth, becoming more self-compassionate is not a linear process. Think of it like climbing a ladder to conquer your fear of heights. You might get up two steps when you realize that you have to pause and catch your breath. You might climb up two more and realize that you have to take a step down because you aren't ready to be up that high yet. Setting yourself up to succeed is an important first step.

Take some time to reflect by answering the following questions:

What feels hard about practicing self-compassion?

Why did you decide to use this workbook?

What are you looking forward to in learning how to be more self-compassionate?

What might your life look like after self-compassion becomes second nature?

REALITY CHECK

This checklist is meant to help you visualize what's going on in your head.

Below is a list of statements that reflect self-judgment and another list that reflects a healthy sense of self-kindness. Place a check mark next to the statements you've thought or said to yourself, even once.

Self-Judgment

☐ I mess up at most things.

☐ I do not measure up to others.

☐ I am awkward.

☐ I'm a failure.

☐ I can't get much right.

☐ I'm uninteresting.

☐ I am not as good as other people.

☐ I'm unsuccessful. I'll never be good at much.

☐ I disappoint myself and others.

☐ I'm weak and scared of too many things.

☐ I'm not very likable.

☐ I'll never have a boyfriend/girlfriend.

☐ I have to do everything perfectly.

☐ I'm going to be rejected.

☐ I'm needy and clingy.

☐ I'm lazy.

☐ I don't have much to add to conversations.

☐ I'm not very smart.

☐ I should get over things more quickly.

☐ I never belong anywhere.

☐ No one wants to be there for me.

☐ I'll always be this way.

☐ I try too hard to fit in.

☐ I'm damaged.

☐ I can't handle difficult emotions.

☐ I beat myself up often.

☐ I'm not good enough.

☐ I'm often left out.

☐ I can't say no.

☐ I'm not especially good at anything.

☐ I don't like my body. I'm unattractive.

☐ I'm not proud of much I've done.

☐ I'm unworthy and unlovable.

☐ I deserve to be given a hard time.

☐ I annoy people.

Self-Kindness

- ☐ I'm successful.
- ☐ I am worthy and lovable.
- ☐ I make mistakes because I'm human.
- ☐ I like my personality.
- ☐ I ask for others to respect me.
- ☐ I'm a likable person.
- ☐ I'm kind and caring
- ☐ I have interesting things to say.
- ☐ I am a good friend.
- ☐ I'm smart.
- ☐ I often act courageously.
- ☐ I deserve good relationships.
- ☐ I comfort myself when I'm sad.
- ☐ It's okay to fail at something.
- ☐ I am unique.
- ☐ I struggle sometimes, and that's okay.
- ☐ I know it's hard to change, but I can do it.
- ☐ I know that being a teen is hard.

- ☐ I'm not liked by everyone, but I like me.
- ☐ I'm good enough.
- ☐ I am proud of myself.
- ☐ I think I'm funny.
- ☐ I believe in myself.
- ☐ I try my best.
- ☐ I know it's impossible to be perfect.
- ☐ I am beautiful as I am.
- ☐ I like who I am as a person.
- ☐ I deserve to ask for help.
- ☐ I know things will work out for me.
- ☐ I feel a sense of belonging.
- ☐ I've gone through some difficult times.
- ☐ I deserve a break when I'm stressed.
- ☐ I can do this.
- ☐ I'm a bit weird, and I like it.
- ☐ I can figure things out.
- ☐ I feel confident in myself.

How many statements did you check off in each section? What did you notice from this exercise? Reflect on whether or not you tend to be kind to yourself.

YOUR BRAIN AND BODY ON STRESS

Let's get familiar with the important role your brain plays in activating—and recovering from—the fight-flight-freeze response, which, as you learned earlier, becomes activated when you are stressed. Once activated, it amplifies fear and other negative emotions and hurts your ability to think and act in a more realistic, helpful way.

The following questions will help you locate where stress sits in your body.

How do you know when you're stressed? Where do you feel it in your body?

How do you know when you are feeling calmer? Where do you feel it in your body?

How do you help bring down your stress response?

Knowing your body's distress signals will alert you that it's time to practice your new self-kindness skills. Next time your body tenses or your heart rate goes up, you'll know it's an opportunity to offer yourself some compassionate attention.

THE STRUGGLE IS REAL

Adolescence is tough! It's a period of transition and rapid growth that leaves teens with so much to stress about. Let's get a reality check on your struggles.

Take a look at this list of typical challenges faced by teens and check off those that you've dealt with or anticipate dealing with.

- ☐ Answering to authority figures
- ☐ Homework and exam stress
- ☐ Body changes/body image issues
- ☐ Friendship issues
- ☐ Pressure to drink/do drugs
- ☐ Heartbreak/rejection
- ☐ Getting made fun of
- ☐ Not fitting in
- ☐ Pressure from parents
- ☐ Waking up early for school
- ☐ Comparing yourself to others
- ☐ Time managing your life
- ☐ Wishing your body was different
- ☐ Loneliness
- ☐ Social media struggles
- ☐ Social anxiety
- ☐ Starting a job

- ☐ Preparing for college
- ☐ Being in clubs and on teams
- ☐ Navigating sexual experiences
- ☐ Bullying
- ☐ Feeling misunderstood
- ☐ Mood changes and difficult emotions
- ☐ Low self-esteem or self-worth
- ☐ Anxiety and/or depression
- ☐ Not knowing who you are
- ☐ Worrying about the future
- ☐ Fights and issues with parents
- ☐ Experiencing failure
- ☐ Trouble sleeping
- ☐ Negative social experiences
- ☐ Shame/embarrassment
- ☐ A traumatic experience

Now choose one of the issues that you checked off and write about: (1) how you coped with this experience, and (2) how you talked to yourself about it. Though space is provided here, feel free to continue in a separate notebook if you've got more to say.

GETTING TO KNOW YOUR INNER CRITIC

There's a reason your mind has let your inner critic run wild. Human brains have a negativity bias. This means that it is much easier for us to focus on negative things than on positive ones. We're quick to believe the critic's message, and we rarely question how well it's doing its job.

Let's get to know this critical voice better by answering the following questions.

What is this critic's purpose in your life? What is its job?

Example: The critical voice makes sure I don't get hurt again.

How does the critic impact your behaviors?

Example: When I tell myself that I'll just be alone forever, it keeps me from allowing myself to have any crushes on anyone.

Has it done a good job at fulfilling its purpose?

Example: It does keep me from getting hurt because I simply don't try—however, that means that I don't even give myself a chance in the first place.

How might a kinder voice fulfill the same purposes you mentioned?

Example: *If I tell myself that I am worthy, I will be braver in talking to my new classmates.*

DRAWING YOUR INNER VOICE

Let's take a break from reading and writing to gain a different kind of perspective on your inner dialogue. You don't have to be artistically inclined to do this exercise. Just draw freely based on what comes to mind. You're welcome to do this on a separate full sheet of paper and use any materials you like in order to fully express yourself.

Draw what your self-critical, fearful voice looks like:

Draw what your self-compassionate, courageous voice sounds like/will sound like:

Jot down a sentence or two noting how you feel about the difference between the two drawings:

_____

_____

_____

NEARING THE FEAR

Negative self-talk and resulting harmful behaviors do serve a purpose, even though they hurt you in the long run. Much of your negativity toward yourself comes not only from learned belief systems but also from fear or worry. The mind believes that self-judgment will keep the fear from coming true. But it is actually self-compassion that allows you to become aware of your fears, validate them, and find helpful ways to vanquish or respond to them.

Place a check mark next to each fear that you have experienced.

☐ Fear of not belonging

☐ Fear of being vulnerable

☐ Fear of not being accepted

☐ Fear of sexual/romantic experiences

☐ Fear of not being worthy

☐ Fear of failure

☐ Fear of disappointing a parent or caregiver

☐ Fear of losing friends

☐ Fear of not finding a romantic partner

☐ Fear of being alone

☐ Fear of not being liked

☐ Fear of being embarrassed

☐ Fear of not being perfect

☐ Fear of confrontation

☐ Fear of making mistakes

☐ Fear of talking to a parent or caregiver about personal problems

☐ Fear of the future

☐ Fear of peer pressure

☐ Fear of bullying

☐ Fear of growing up

☐ Fear of social situations

☐ Fear of being too different

☐ Fear of rejection

☐ Fear of _____

☐ Fear of _____

☐ Fear of _____

Now choose one of the fears that you checked off and answer the following questions about it:

How does it keep you stuck or impact you?

Example: *I am afraid of not being perfect. As a result, I am constantly pushing myself beyond my limits to get perfect grades. I spend every moment worrying about the next exam or assignment. I tell myself not to be lazy in order to keep this fear from coming true.*

What thoughts or behaviors make these fears bigger?

Example: I constantly remind myself that if I don't do the best job in the whole class, my parents will be angry with me. I also spend so much of my day worrying about what grade I'll get after I take an exam.

What kind of thoughts or behaviors could make these fears become smaller?

Example: I can remind myself that no one can be perfect and that it's okay to just be "good enough." I can also talk to my parents about my worry that they won't be happy with me if I don't do perfectly.

Once we've gotten near some of the fears lurking around, we can change the way we respond when we get scared, evoking a more self-compassionate response.

PASSIVE AND ACTIVE SELF-COMPASSION

There are different ways to practice self-compassion when you're having a rough time—some are more passive, some more active.

In this exercise, you will focus on both types of self-compassion practices. Under each type of practice, write down at least two examples of self-compassionate actions that you think would be helpful for you.

Remember, this exercise is about what you authentically need and what will be kind and healthy for you in the long term, not just in the immediate moment. For example, eating a box of cookies might be instantly satisfying but could lead to a bellyache in the long run and may not be a sustainable self-compassion practice. These can be phrases, thoughts, or actions. You may not have yet discovered a practice for a particular type of self-compassionate action, and that's okay. Come back to this exercise later, and feel free to keep adding more as you learn more about what helps you in tough moments.

Passive Self-Compassion *(How to offer yourself care and be connected to the present moment when you're in pain)*

Comforting (Offering yourself support for emotional needs)

1.

2.

Soothing (Offering yourself support for physical calm)

1.

2.

Validating (Offering yourself support to help you feel understood/less alone)

1.

2.

Active Self-Compassion *(How to bravely see the truth of your experience and protect yourself)*

Protecting (Creating boundaries and space for yourself; fierceness and empowerment)

1.

2.

Providing (Knowing and giving yourself what you truly need; balancing it with others' needs)

1.

2.

Motivating (Encouragement when you're stuck; finding ways to push yourself with kindness)

1. _____

2. _____

TALKING WITH FUTURE YOU

This is a free-writing exercise where "Future You" is self-compassionate, courageous, and vulnerable, writing to "Present You," who isn't quite there yet. What does Future You remind you of? What kind of wisdom do they have? What do they say to encourage your self-compassion practice? How do they validate what you're going through?

```
Dear Present You,

I know you are not very happy right now. I notice
how you always beat yourself up for any mistakes
you make. I want you to know that it's okay to
make mistakes. One day you will see that being kind
to yourself will make you happier than you have
ever been.

Love,

Future You
```

MINDFULNESS PRACTICES

MINDFUL MIND

A mindful mind is a calmer, happier, and clearer mind. It pays close attention to the present moment without getting caught up in whatever might be stressful or painful. Mindfulness invites you to take a breath when something is overwhelming you and helps make the pain smaller and less scary. When you become more mindful, you begin noticing that your brain gives you a lot of thoughts—and not all of them are very helpful or even true! When you realize this, you are better able to make different decisions when you approach difficult situations.

The following is a list of the components of mindfulness. Read them over and place checks next to those you'd like to practice more.

COMPONENTS OF A MINDFUL MIND

☐ **Nonjudgment.** Being an impartial observer of your experience. You no longer label thoughts and emotions as good, bad, fair, unfair, etc. You simply observe them. (For example, when you are having a thought or emotion, simply label it as if you were watching the clouds go by. "Ah! A thought. Ah! A feeling. There's another one!")

☐ **Beginner's mind.** Approaching a situation as if you were a child seeing it for the first time. (For example: What would a child say to their first not-so-great grade if they didn't know what it meant not to do so great on an exam?)

☐ **Gratitude.** Choosing to be thankful instead of allowing guilt and shame into your mind. (For example, instead of making yourself feel bad for a mistake you made, choose to be grateful you learned something from it.)

☐ **Affectionate attention.** Noticing what is happening with warmth and gentleness. (For example, when you're feeling bad, notice your sadness and tenderly address it as you might a tiny puppy.)

☐ **Curiosity.** Wondering and inquiring about your thoughts, feelings, and life situations. (For example, a scientist finds a bacterium. She doesn't know what it does. If she immediately acts afraid of it, she will be unable to study it to learn more about it and share that knowledge.)

☐ **Letting go.** Allowing yourself to release something that isn't helping you. (For example, you know how you often wish that a particular person wouldn't hurt you? Letting that go is like releasing a balloon you've been clenching very tightly and just allowing it to float up into the wind. Your hand gets to relax, and you simply watch the balloon float away. You don't need it.)

☐ **Acceptance.** Validating and acknowledging things as they are. Accepting what is or has happened as the truth—even if you don't like it. (For example, when you accept that you failed a test, you no longer replay what you could have done differently. You acknowledge that you cannot go back in time, and you simply accept that you failed. Now you can look toward doing better on the next test.)

☐ **Humor.** Laughing or creating humor in a stressful moment to help your mind not take it so seriously. (For example, perhaps you embarrassed yourself in front of friends. Can you imagine that moment happening on a funny TV show?)

☐ **Patience.** Knowing deep in your heart that things happen at their own pace and not getting upset by this. (For example, your body may be developing at a different pace than your peers' bodies, and you're feeling behind. Remind yourself to be patient. Yours will do its thing in time.)

☐ **Openness.** Not shutting down painful or unpleasant experiences, but rather staying open to them and learning ways to help yourself through them. (For example, when it feels like sadness from a rejection is too much to bear, turn your attention to how that emotion happens in your body instead of wishing it would go away.)

Now choose one or two of the practices that you checked off and write about how they might help you with your self-compassion.

Know that as you're learning how to be more mindful, you can always turn to this list for ideas on responding to difficult experiences. Does a situation need more patience? Less judgment? Do you need to approach it with humor to lighten it up? Pick one of these to practice each week. This would be a good time to start a self-compassion journal and write about your experiences.

MINDFUL MOMENTS: YOUR FIVE SENSES

One of the simple tools for staying mindful involves your five senses. If your mind wanders, you can bring your attention back to the present moment by noticing what you see, hear, smell, feel, and/or taste. With this method, you can create a mindful moment any time you feel overwhelmed, anxious, or sad or just want to get your mind out of the past or future.

Let's try it out by answering the following questions. (Make sure that whatever you note down is something you can objectively observe—without an opinion or extra meaning. For example, "I see a tree," not, "I see a tree that I really like.")

What do you see?

What do you hear?

What do you smell?

What do you feel?

What do you taste? (Perhaps grab a small snack for this part of the exercise.)

Now close your eyes and observe your body using your five senses. Notice what you feel inside and on your body.

What do you notice happens to your thoughts when you keep bringing your attention to what is happening in your body and surroundings? Does the critical voice quiet down for a bit?

Try this exercise in different environments to see how it feels—for example, in the classroom if your mind wanders during an exam, or when you're on a walk and you want a break from thinking your usual thoughts.

NAME IT AND TAME IT

Has your brain ever gotten stuck in a loop where you think about the same thing over and over? There's a simple skill for helping you get out of this loop, and it's called "labeling." When a thought comes up in your mind, you simply label it as a "thought." Likewise, when a strong feeling comes on, just label it a "feeling." This takes away the judgment; you're not saying these thoughts and feelings are negative or positive—they're just thoughts and feelings.

Labeling helps our brain categorize information and then decide whether or not to be threatened. A story that you tell yourself (for example, "Molly will never like me") will be much more threatening to your brain than an objective label (for example, "I have a thought . . . that Molly will never like me"). When you make a little space between yourself and the "thought" or the "feeling," you will get less overwhelmed by an emotion or situation. Your brain gives you an average of 70,000 thoughts a day—you can't possibly believe and listen to every single one.

FUN FACTS:

Thoughts are not facts!

An emotional response lasts 90 seconds. Rest assured, emotions are not a permanent catastrophe, and they will pass.

Try This:

Close your eyes, and imagine you can see what is happening in your mind. You can set a timer for three minutes for your first try. As soon as you notice your brain is thinking, simply label it "thinking." As soon as you notice that you are feeling something, label it "feeling." The goal isn't to catch every single thought or feeling—that would be impossible—but to get into the habit of naming and taming the contents of your mind. Don't worry if this is hard to do. There's no success or failure here, simply the intention to give yourself a break from negative or stressful experiences.

Now take a few minutes to write about this experience. What was it like? What was tough about it? Where did you notice your mind wander to?

Continued >

The more you practice this exercise, the easier it will become to stay present and notice when your mind is wandering. Think of this as yoga for your brain. Soon enough, the thoughts and emotions that you couldn't shake won't feel as intense or stay as long.

BEING AWARE OF BREATH

Your breath is a powerful tool—it does keep you alive, after all! Learning how to use it in a more effective way can help with relaxation, self-soothing, and reduction in the stress response. Think about what happens when you're afraid, angry, or anxious. You tend to breathe shallowly or too quickly or even hold your breath without realizing. Let's learn an effective, more compassionate way to use our breath.

Here are two simple exercises that involve being mindful of your breath. You can use them to soothe yourself, become more present, or just take a pause in your day.

For this exercise you can sit in a chair or on a cushion, stand, or even lie in your bed.

Deep Breathing:

Close your eyes if you feel comfortable doing so. Focus on your breath; notice it going in and out.

1. Breathe in through your nose for the count of 1-2-3-4. Take in air, and feel it in your nose and going into your belly and lungs.

2. Breathe out through your mouth as if you were breathing into a straw (through a small opening in your lips) for the count of 1-2-3-4-5-6-7-8. The goal is to breathe out slower and with more control than when you breathe in. Each time, try to push air out even slower.

3. Alternate between steps 1 and 2 for however long you like, aiming for at least five minutes.

TIPS:

We are used to breathing just into our lungs. Learning how to fill your belly with air will deepen the breathing and help you feel calmer. Don't worry, it takes practice. Hold your hand on your belly if it helps you to feel it move out as you breathe in.

When you notice your mind drifting off to other thoughts or negative self-talk, gently remind yourself, "I'm just breathing now," and bring your focus back to the breathing. Your mind will continue to wander; don't judge or criticize yourself—just remind yourself that you're paying attention to your breath.

Breathing in Color:

This exercise is meant to combine deep breathing (what you learned in the previous exercise) with visualization that can help create a greater sense of calm and focus.

1. Pick a color that represents a state of kindness and calm to you (for example, light blue). You can be specific, as it will help make the visualization more vivid. Pick another color that represents a state of stress or difficulty to you (for example, dark orange).

2. Close your eyes. Breathe in, and as you do so, imagine the air you're breathing is the color you chose to represent calm. Feel the calm-colored air flow into your nose, lungs, and belly, filling you with a state of relaxation. On the slower out-breath, imagine that you are exhaling the stress-colored air. As you breathe it out, picture the stress leaving your body. Picture the calm-colored air replacing the stress-colored spaces in your body.

3. Alternate between steps 1 and 2 for at least five minutes.

TIPS:

You may create a color on your own or use a color of a familiar object that brings you calm and joy. For example, if you have a favorite blanket that is light yellow, you can use that to strengthen your visualization.

You can practice either of these breathing exercises for 1 minute or 20 minutes. Use your breath as a way to ground yourself in the present moment or as a way to help counter a stress response with a relaxation response.

BECOMING CURIOUS

Curiosity is an aspect of mindfulness that can change the way we respond to scary, stressful, and painful situations. We can learn to change from feeling threatened to being inquisitive and curious about our internal and external world. When we judge our thoughts, emotions, and situations as good or bad, we tend to suffer more. When we wonder and act like an explorer of our world, we see things more clearly and calmly. Curiosity is a gentler and more compassionate choice.

Let's practice changing fearfulness into curiosity by exploring these five situations.

Example situation: You failed a test, and you're given the chance to take it again.

Fear response: I already failed it once. I'm sure I'll fail it again.

Curious response: I wonder where it is that I went wrong on this exam and what I can study to try to do better.

Which response do you think will motivate you and make it more likely that you might get a better grade and why?

Situation 1:

You want to go to the school dance, and you don't have someone to go with.

Fear response:

Curious response:

How does the curious response make you feel about the dance now?

Situation 2:

Your parents grounded you because you stayed out too late.

    Fear response:

    Curious response:

How does responding with a curious mind soften the experience of being grounded?

Situation 3:

You tried on a piece of clothing at a store that you really liked in your usual size and it didn't fit you.

    Fear response:

    Curious response:

Is there something that feels difficult about responding to your body with curiosity?

Situation 4:

Online, you saw that two of your close friends were hanging out without you.

    Fear response:

    Curious response:

What can you say to yourself to feel better when you're feeling left out?

Situation 5:

Your turn. Fill in your own.

Fear response:

Curious response:

How does the curious response make you feel?

TIP:

Now that you've learned how to respond with curiosity instead of fear, I encourage you to use this approach next time you have an opportunity and note it in your self-compassion journal.

RADICAL ACCEPTANCE

When you "radically accept" something difficult in your life, it doesn't mean that you are giving up or giving in. It just means that you can see reality for how it is and accept it wholeheartedly. A lot of pain comes from convincing yourself that things aren't as they are or that you can change something that you cannot.

How Humans Tend to React to a Distressing Situation:

1. They try to change the circumstances.

2. They try to change their behavior to fit the circumstances.

3. They continue to feel miserable or bad.

4. They accept the circumstances.

Three Parts to Radical Acceptance:

1. Accepting that your reality is what it is.

2. Accepting that the difficult event or situation causing you pain has a cause.

3. Accepting life can be worth living even though painful things happen.

In each numbered space in the following exercise, list an event that happened in your life that has caused you stress or pain. Explain why it is difficult to accept. Write your acceptance statement(s). Take some time to practice saying the acceptance statement out loud or writing it over and over. As you say it or write it, take deep breaths, be gentle, and really feel yourself accepting the truth. Imagine your stomach untightening and your chest opening up to make way for more air.

Example event: My parents are getting divorced.

Why it is difficult to accept: I wish they hadn't decided to get divorced. I can't stop thinking about what I could have done to keep it from happening. I am so resentful of them for doing this to me. I feel sick all the time.

Acceptance statement(s): I accept that my parents are divorcing. I accept that they will not be together. I accept that it is their decision.

Event 1:

Why it is difficult to accept:

Acceptance statement(s):

Event 2:

Why it is difficult to accept:

Acceptance statement(s):

Event 3:

Why it is difficult to accept:

Acceptance statement(s):

Event 4:

Why it is difficult to accept:

Acceptance statement(s):

Event 5:

Why it is difficult to accept:

Acceptance statement(s):

WORKING WITH DIFFICULT EMOTIONS

FEELING THE PAIN

Have you ever felt desperate to avoid feeling pain? Although negative feelings are an inevitable part of life, we tend to run from them like crazy. They don't feel so good, do they? Self-compassion can help you sit with a difficult emotion and pay attention to it in a different way, instead of letting it run the show.

Place a check mark next to any painful feelings that you have experienced.

Mad	Sad	Scared	Disgusted
☐ Accused	☐ Depressed	☐ Afraid	☐ Embarrassed
☐ Angry	☐ Disappointed	☐ Anxious	☐ Exposed
☐ Bitter	☐ Discouraged	☐ Cautious	☐ Guilty
☐ Defensive	☐ Grief-stricken	☐ Confused	☐ Ignored
☐ Frustrated	☐ Gloomy	☐ Frightened	☐ Inadequate
☐ Furious	☐ Hopeless	☐ Lost	☐ Incompetent
☐ Hostile	☐ Let Down	☐ Helpless	☐ Inferior
☐ Impatient	☐ Lonely	☐ Hesitant	☐ Insignificant
☐ Offended	☐ Heartbroken	☐ Insecure	☐ Sick
☐ Pestered	☐ Miserable	☐ Nervous	☐ Shamed
☐ Resistant	☐ Neglected	☐ Reserved	☐ Squashed
☐ Revengeful	☐ Pessimistic	☐ Uncomfortable	☐ Stupid
☐ Used	☐ Resentful	☐ Useless	☐ Ugly
☐ Violated	☐ Tearful	☐ Threatened	☐ Unaccepted

Feel free to add any other difficult feelings to the list that you have experienced.

Pick three painful feelings and write about how they affect your body, thoughts, and behaviors. Becoming more mindful of how they make your body feel and how you typically react to them can allow you to know when you need to send some self-compassion your way to acknowledge and ease the pain.

1. _____

_____

_____

_____

2. _____

_____

_____

_____

_____

3. _____

_____

_____

_____

_____

Stay tuned for exercises that can help you deal with specific difficult and painful emotions.

SHUTTING OUT SHAME

Practicing self-compassion is an antidote to feeling shame. Shame is defined by shame researcher and expert Brené Brown as the "intensely painful feeling or experience of believing that we are flawed and therefore unworthy of love and belonging" and is behind so many of our unhelpful behaviors. Shame makes us believe we are unworthy, unlovable, and unacceptable the way we are—that the things we've done or failed to do somehow make us undeserving of connection, love, and friendship. Have you ever felt this way for even a moment? Shame says, "I am bad." You are not bad! That's just shame getting in the way of the truth.

You might feel that shame deserves blame, but it is an innocent emotion that comes from the wish to be loved and accepted.

You might feel that shame is only your own scary emotion, but it is universal to all humans.

You might feel that shame will last forever, but it is momentary, like all emotions.

Write about one time you remember experiencing shame. What did it feel like? How did it make you behave?

Anytime you start to feel shame in the future, use the following steps to prompt you into substituting self-compassion.

1. Label it as shame when you catch yourself thinking that you are bad, unlovable, unworthy, etc. Say to yourself:
   "Oh! That's shame" or "Woah! There's shame again."

2. Remind yourself that it's just an emotion. Soften your body, and take a deep breath. Say to yourself:
   "I'm feeling shame because I have a normal human desire to feel belonging, acceptance, and love."

3. Close your eyes and picture the faces of people closest to you as well as strangers all over the world, knowing that they all experience shame. Say to yourself:

   "Wow, I know that nearly every human feels this painful emotion. It's part of our human experience. I'm not alone in that."

4. Begin to observe, much like a scientist would, the way shame feels in your body and mind. Try not to judge it or fuel it with more thoughts. See how it changes over time. What does it make you want to do? Yell? Hide? Harm yourself?

5. Place a hand over your heart, and feel the weight of your body wherever you are. Say to yourself:

   "May I know I am worthy."
   "May I know I am lovable."
   "May I know I am human."

6. Shame typically makes us want to choose fight (anger/resentment), flight (ruminate), or freeze (hide out). Think of what the shame is making you want to do. Now think of something that is the complete opposite. For example, if your boyfriend broke up with you, and you are ignoring your friends' texts, can you practice step 5 and then choose to text them back?

Take some time to reflect on and write about how this exercise was for you. Were you able to label the shame and observe it for a little while? What was difficult about this exercise? What do you see as the benefits of using self-compassion to combat your shame?

COOLING THE FLAMES OF ANGER

Anger is a normal emotion, but it can be helpful to know that it is often secondary to something else that's fueling it. For example, someone may have been unkind to you, and so your painful feelings of shame and rejection cause anger to flare up and take center stage. There are healthy ways to be angry, but sometimes it can really take over your mind and body. Let's learn how to meet our anger with healthier coping skills and self-compassion.

Write down an example of something that is making you angry now or has made you angry in the past:

When you take the time to examine the anger, you can act instead of react, which will be a more self-compassionate response. Follow these steps, and answer all the questions, to explore a new way to respond when anger arises.

Build Self-Awareness:

What is making you angry? Why are you feeling this way? Are there any other feelings? Where do you feel anger in your body?

What does the anger make you want to do?

Develop Potential Responses:

Think of at least three ways you can respond to this anger:

Think through the Consequences:

What might be the consequences of each of the responses you came up with?

Make Your Decision:

Now that you've taken some more time, you can choose a solution that will most likely be helpful and effective. What is your best choice? If you've already had your knee-jerk reaction, what can you do next time?

Meet Anger with Mindfulness:

When you are mindful of a difficult emotion, you can pause to create space between what's making you angry and the way you respond. This allows you to slow down instead of being immediately reactive. Here are some more ways to cool the flames.

* Put a hand over the area where you feel the anger, and imagine yourself breathing cool air into that area.

* Gently label what is happening: "This is anger." "My stomach is tight." "My heart is pounding." "My face is hot."

* Count your deep breaths: Use your fingers to tap the counts of each breath.

* Grounded feet: Focus your awareness on your feet on the ground, and explore the sensations. Ground yourself in the present moment.

Based on what you've tried with your new skills, what feels the most useful for you to cope with anger?

Next time you feel angry, return to this exercise and follow the steps again.

SITTING WITH SADNESS

What you ignore comes at you more. What you feel, you can heal. Sadness can be a difficult emotion to bear, and when it becomes intense, you might be at risk for depression. Let's learn a kinder and more helpful way to sit with our sad emotions without letting them take over.

Write down something that is making you sad now or has made you sad in the past.

Why are you feeling this way? Are there any other feelings? Where do you feel sadness in your body?

What does the sadness make you want to do? How do you usually respond to your sadness?

Write down a few of your current beliefs about sadness. Do you believe it's normal and okay to feel sad? Do others feel that way, too? What do you think others need when they are sad?

Now it's time to meet sadness with self-kindness, common humanity, and mindfulness.

Write down three kind things you can say to yourself when you are feeling sad. For example, "I can let myself feel sad. There's no need to beat myself up right now."

Write down three helpful things you can do that will be comforting to you when you are sad. For example, "I can ask my older sister to watch a movie with me."

Name one or more people you care about who have felt sad before. What have you said to them when they felt that way?

Practice accepting the sadness by writing down or saying acceptance statements. For example, "This is sadness." "I accept that I am feeling sad." "I accept that I am down right now."

When sadness is taking over, you can practice shifting your attention to make room for other experiences. Write down three positive things that are going on in your life that have nothing to do with your experience of sadness. For example, "I have two awesome friends I hang out with every day at lunch."

REBOUNDING FROM REJECTION

Life is full of rejection—and it really hurts! Why? Science has shown that the way the brain responds to rejection is similar to the way it responds to physical pain. No wonder it hurts so much.

We tend to treat physical pain with immediate care so that it can heal as quickly as possible. You can learn to respond in the same caring way to the pain of rejection. When you respond to rejection with self-compassion, you will take it less personally, spend less time stuck on negative thoughts, and bounce back more quickly.

Let's look at the five types of rejection you may have experienced. Under each type, answer the following questions:

A. What are some ways in which you've been rejected in this area?

B. How do you feel when it happens?

C. How do you typically respond when it happens?

D. What are two self-compassionate ways you can respond if it happens again?

Academic rejection (for example, not getting into an honors class or a club; getting a bad grade)

A.

B.

C.

D.

Familial rejection (for example, a parent or caregiver ignoring a story you're telling; being neglected or abandoned; having your feelings dismissed)

A.

B.

C.

D.

Social rejection (for example, not getting invited to a party; being bullied; a rumor being spread about you; a friend group pushing you out)

A.

B.

C.

D.

Rejection in a relationship (for example, a partner refusing to open up, cheating on you, being unkind to you, or breaking up with you)

A.

B.

C.

D.

Romantic rejection (for example, the person you ask out saying no; your crush not reciprocating feelings)

A.

B.

C.

D.

LOCATING EMOTIONS IN YOUR BODY

Our brains tend to focus a lot on the "self." That means when you're feeling sad about something, you tend to start thinking more and more about it. You start telling yourself a story about the painful way you're feeling (more on that later). One important thing to remember is that every emotion is accompanied by changes in your body and in the sensations you experience. Knowing how to shift your focus to where pain and emotion are in the body is a more self-compassionate way of coping with difficult moments.

Let's say that when you start feeling sadness or rage, you want to resort to self-harm, send mean texts, or yell at your parents. This is your moment to take a step back and try a different response.

This exercise is designed to help you cope more compassionately and effectively with your difficult emotions in real time, as they arise. However, you can participate even if you aren't currently feeling a strong emotion. Just try to remember a difficult emotion you have experienced in the past.

1. Find a place where you can sit or lie down comfortably and won't be disturbed. Remind yourself that the thoughts will be there, and you can come back to them—you don't have to worry about them now.

2. Close your eyes and take a few deep breaths. Your mind will wander to the events surrounding the emotion. Ask yourself, "What am I feeling right now?" Once you answer, take another deep breath. Label the emotion that you are feeling—for example, "This is rage."

3. Start to notice where you are feeling this in your body. Imagine you have control over a spotlight, and you need to shine it on whatever part of your body is feeling this emotion. Label in your mind where and what you're feeling. For example, "My stomach is very tight. My face is hot. My hands are shaking, and my body feels restless. My face just became hotter, and my jaw is clenching."

4. Continue to observe how the emotion feels in your body. Do your best to stay focused on what is present in the moment, even when your thoughts wander. You'll likely remember another painful incident or something else that conjures up strong emotions. Your goal is to shift the spotlight away from the thoughts and to the feelings in your body.

5. Continue to observe your emotion, checking in every so often to see if it has changed. Perhaps it got more or less intense. Notice where it has changed in your body, too.

6. When you are aware that the emotion has lessened in intensity, you can end the exercise. Take a few deep breaths, and slowly open your eyes. Stay still for a few moments. Check in with how you're feeling.

Reflection: How did you feel when you first started this exercise? Where did you feel the emotion in your body? What was difficult about this exercise? What was helpful? What changes did you notice from start to finish?

THOUGHTS AND LANGUAGE

IDENTIFYING NEGATIVE THOUGHTS

The following exercise is designed to help you get better at catching your negative thoughts as they come up. This will help you question how they affect you instead of simply believing them. Instead, you can choose to reframe, accept, or let it go.

Write down three negative thoughts you have recently had. For example, "I'm a bad friend."

How do these thoughts make you feel? For example, "I feel alone and like a bad person."

What do these thoughts make you do or want to do? For example, "I want to hide and avoid going to school."

How do you think these negative thoughts help you? For example, "If I know I'm a bad friend, I won't bother getting to know people, since it won't work out anyway."

One way to keep this practice in your everyday life is to have your self-compassion journal nearby to jot down negative thoughts as they come to you. This is how you become more mindful about how negatively your inner dialogue operates. Once you catch these thoughts in action, you can more easily replace them with more self-compassionate responses.

IDENTIFYING CORE BELIEFS

Core beliefs are the strongly held, deep-seated thoughts and assumptions we hold about ourselves, others, and the world around us. These beliefs are reinforced because we tend to focus on information that supports them and ignore evidence that disproves them. Some core beliefs can negatively influence the way we interpret what happens in our lives and the things people say to us. These negative core beliefs become harmful when we accept them as fact, whether or not they are true.

Let's identify some of your core beliefs. Place a check mark next to those that currently apply to you.

- ☐ I am a failure.
- ☐ I am a loser.
- ☐ I am flawed.
- ☐ I am imperfect.
- ☐ I can't succeed.
- ☐ I am nothing.
- ☐ I am invisible.
- ☐ I am awkward.
- ☐ I can't control anything.
- ☐ I am stupid.
- ☐ I am all alone.
- ☐ I am unimportant.
- ☐ I am unacceptable.
- ☐ I don't matter.
- ☐ I don't have the power to keep myself healthy.
- ☐ I can't get it right.

- ☐ I am afraid.
- ☐ I finish last.
- ☐ I am a mistake.
- ☐ I don't deserve anything.
- ☐ I don't deserve to be happy.
- ☐ I can't do it.
- ☐ I can't do anything on my own.
- ☐ I am insignificant.
- ☐ I am broken.
- ☐ I will inevitably be rejected.
- ☐ I am ugly.
- ☐ I have ruined my whole life.
- ☐ Nothing works for me.
- ☐ I have to do everything perfectly.
- ☐ I can't change.

- ☐ I am inferior.
- ☐ I don't know who I really am.
- ☐ I don't exist.
- ☐ I am unlikable.
- ☐ I am unattractive.
- ☐ I am needy.
- ☐ I must struggle in order to succeed.
- ☐ I will lose.
- ☐ My needs are not important.
- ☐ I don't deserve success.
- ☐ I don't trust anyone.
- ☐ I am crazy.
- ☐ I am unfixable.
- ☐ I don't deserve to be loved.
- ☐ I am guilty.
- ☐ People are untrustworthy.

- [ ] I have to make people happy.
- [ ] I am incompetent.
- [ ] I don't have the energy.
- [ ] I don't deserve closeness.
- [ ] I will fail.
- [ ] People will betray me.
- [ ] I am weak.
- [ ] I can't handle anything.
- [ ] I must always please in order to have love.
- [ ] I am not good enough.
- [ ] I am bad.
- [ ] I will inevitably be abandoned by someone I love.
- [ ] If I don't excel, then I am inferior and worthless.

- [ ] I am always left out.
- [ ] I can't be me.
- [ ] It's my fault.
- [ ] If I don't do it, no one will.
- [ ] I am not lovable.
- [ ] I might get hurt.
- [ ] I am not enough.
- [ ] I can't say no.
- [ ] Failing is unacceptable.
- [ ] I am not worthy of a happy and healthy life.
- [ ] I never get my way.
- [ ] I don't deserve to be cared for.
- [ ] I am not safe.
- [ ] I am destined to be a victim.

- [ ] If I can't do it perfectly, then I'd better not do it.
- [ ] I am not special.
- [ ] If I make a mistake, it means I'm a failure.
- [ ] I am always wrong.
- [ ] I am worthless.
- [ ] I am powerless.
- [ ] I cannot be myself.
- [ ] I am useless.
- [ ] I don't measure up to others.
- [ ] I am unsuccessful.
- [ ] I cannot be healed.
- [ ] If I experience emotions, I will lose control.
- [ ] I don't belong.

Reflection: How do you feel about how many you checked off? Do you believe that you can change these limiting beliefs? How do you think self-compassion practice will help you think differently about yourself?

Self-compassion helps you see yourself with a more balanced and kind perspective, eventually allowing your mind to adopt more realistic and helpful beliefs about yourself. Remember that countless other teens have thought these things about themselves—you're not alone.

CHANGING CORE BELIEFS

Beliefs are thoughts—and you are *not* your thoughts. You don't have to believe everything you think. Thoughts are not facts!

On each first line in the following exercise, write down one of the negative core beliefs that you checked off in the previous exercise. Then, think of an experience that shows this belief is *not completely true all the time*, and write it down on the second line. Next, create a new core belief that is true and more self-compassionate, and write it on the third line. Additional space is provided so you can practice with the other core beliefs that you checked off.

Example:

Negative core belief: I have to do everything perfectly.

Experience: I got a bad grade on my English test, and my friends didn't care or think any less of me.

New balanced core belief: I am imperfect, like all humans. It's okay to make mistakes. Nearly everyone gets bad grades.

Negative core belief:

Experience:

New balanced core belief:

Negative core belief:

Experience:

New balanced core belief:

Negative core belief:

Experience:

New balanced core belief:

Negative core belief:

Experience:

New balanced core belief:

Negative core belief:

Experience:

New balanced core belief:

Remember: It's all about being more compassionate toward yourself. As you get better at catching your negative core beliefs in action, you'll be able to start replacing them with your new, more positive beliefs.

TIP:

Write your new balanced core belief on a card and carry it around with you as a constant reminder.

WORKING WITH WORRY

Worry is a common type of thinking that most teens (and many adults) engage in. You might worry about something that happened in the past or something that might happen in the future. Worrying can be exhausting and isn't very helpful.

This exercise will help you identify worry thoughts and come up with more compassionate and thoughtful ways of dealing with them. For "previous response," write down how you respond to this worry right now. For "self-compassionate response," write down your new, kinder way of responding.

Example: I am worried about how well I did on the math exam.

Can I do something about it? Yes/No

Previous response: I am spending every moment that I'm not in school thinking about this. I'm constantly trying to come up with a solution.

Self-compassionate response: Worrying about something I cannot change only makes me anxious. I will choose to be kind to myself even if I get a bad grade and try to do better next time.

I am worried about:

Can I do something about it?   Yes/No

Previous response:

Self-compassionate response:

I am worried about:

Can I do something about it?   Yes/No

Previous response:

Self-compassionate response:

I am worried about:

Can I do something about it?   Yes/No

Previous response:

Self-compassionate response:

As you can see from this exercise, there are self-compassionate ways to deal with your worries. You don't have to live in a state of worry anymore.

CHALLENGING THE CATASTROPHE

Catastrophic thinking is the tendency to think of the worst-case scenario or jump to an extreme opinion about yourself or your situation—particularly one that hasn't happened yet. This thinking trap is meant to protect you, but in reality, it builds fear and makes you less equipped to handle what comes your way. Sometimes it may seem as if the worst is definitely going to happen—but more often than not, it is very unlikely.

Let's challenge this catastrophic way of thinking with this series of questions:

What catastrophe are you thinking about?

How likely is it that this will happen? Has it happened before?

What is the worst-case scenario if this catastrophe does happen?

What would a friend say to you about this worry?

If the worst were to happen, how might you cope? Are there mindfulness or self-compassion skills you could use?

What compassionate or positive thing could you say to yourself now as you think about this catastrophe? What do you need to hear?

Remember, you can go through this process any time you catch yourself thinking of the worst-case scenario.

SLIPPING PAST SELF-DOUBT

Have you ever lacked confidence in your ability to do something? Have you been unsure that you could be successful? If the answer is yes, then you are part of a big group of fellow teens who have felt this way, too. Self-doubt—often combined with low self-esteem—can keep you from doing the things that you know in your heart you want to do. On top of that, many teens beat themselves up for not being brave enough to do something, which only further hurts their confidence. Let's get to know self-doubt and find more self-compassionate ways to address it.

Place a check mark next to what self-doubt sounds like for you:

☐ I'm not sure I can do this.

☐ I probably won't get into the band.

☐ I don't think my parents will take me seriously if I tell them.

☐ I don't think I deserve to get another chance.

☐ I don't think he could like me.

☐ I don't think I'm good enough to make it on varsity.

☐ I'm not as good as he is at soccer.

☐ I don't think she'd want to hang out with me.

Name three situations in which you have experienced a lack of confidence and doubted yourself or your abilities.

> *Example:* I wanted to ask a new friend I met to come over to my house, but I was worried she'd say no.

Pick one of those three situations. What was your response when you began doubting yourself? What was the outcome of the self-doubt?

> *Example:* I spent a few days really anxious about the prospect of asking her, coming up with scenarios of how she could say no. I didn't end up asking because I felt too stuck in my fear.

What do you think could have helped you feel more confident in that situation?

> *Example:* I often believe that I'm not fun to be around. I have two good friends who really like me, and I probably could have reminded myself of that. I also could have used better self-talk to build more confidence in myself.

What are some more self-compassionate ways to respond to self-doubt the next time around?

Example: I can notice when I'm not being very kind to myself. I can tell myself that I am a good person and people do like being around me. I can recognize that my self-doubtful inner monologue is giving me some unhelpful information. I can also ask my close friend for support in reminding me that it's okay to feel scared of rejection but that I can handle it even if someone says no.

Do you have any doubts about what will happen if you choose self-compassion in these situations?

Example: Yes, like what if I'm kind to myself and that actually keeps me from seeing that I could easily be rejected? I'm afraid that being self-compassionate to overcome self-doubt will just make me overconfident.

Remind yourself why it's important to choose a self-compassionate response to move past your self-doubt.

THE STORIES WE TELL OURSELVES

Our minds constantly give meaning to our experiences by creating stories to explain those experiences. Unfortunately, those stories are not necessarily facts.

This exercise focuses on teaching you how to shift from a *narrative* (story) mode to an *experiential* (in-the-moment) mode. Science shows that when we operate in the narrative mode, we tend to be more self-critical, but when we're in the experiential mode, we tend to be more self-accepting.

When we're in the narrative mode, we tend to think about and analyze our emotional experiences, getting caught up in thoughts and self-evaluation.

When we're in the experiential mode, on the other hand, we tend to notice and stay with what is happening in our bodies as we are going through an emotional experience.

Minds like to label things as good/bad, pleasant/unpleasant, like/dislike. Our beliefs influence the kinds of stories we tell. If we're in a bad mood, for example, we are more likely to think a TV show we might otherwise find funny is not funny at all. Noticing your thought stream and labeling it as a story you're telling yourself is a great mindfulness practice. It also makes room for you to start paying attention to what is actually happening in your body and gets you out of your head.

Let's look at some of your experiences and break them down in terms of observable facts, feelings, stories you tell yourself, and how your body responds. Try to complete all five sets, but know that this is a tough practice, so don't worry if you struggle.

Example:

Observable fact: At lunch today, no one laughed at my joke.

I'm feeling: Sad and rejected.

The story I'm telling myself is: My friends think I'm awkward and unfunny. I hate that they never laugh at my jokes. I'll just stop talking at lunch altogether. I wonder if they talk about how weird I am behind my back. I'm sure they do.

Where I feel it in my body: I'm feeling it in the pit of my stomach. My chest is tight, and I'm noticing that I'm holding my breath.

Observable fact 1:

I'm feeling:

The story I'm telling myself is:

Where I feel it in my body:

Observable fact 2:

I'm feeling:

The story I'm telling myself is:

Where I feel it in my body:

Observable fact 3:

I'm feeling:

The story I'm telling myself is:

Where I feel it in my body:

Observable fact 4:

I'm feeling:

The story I'm telling myself is:

Where I feel it in my body:

> TIP:
>
> The goal of this exercise is to learn how to catch yourself in the story and move your attention to your body. Your mind will wander, and it's your job to keep asking yourself, "Wait, what is my body doing right now? Where do I feel this pain?"

CHANGING SHOULD AND CAN'T

Should and *can't* are two examples of limiting and judgmental language. When you tell yourself you should do—or should have done—something, you imply that there is or was a better option that you didn't choose. This isn't very self-compassionate. When you tell yourself that you can't do something, it's important to examine if that's really true. Is it that you can't or that you're afraid to? Or is it that it's just really hard to do? Use the common scenarios here to practice changing from *should* and *can't* to self-compassionate language.

Rewrite each of the following six statements from a more self-compassionate, realistic, and positive perspective.

Example:

Should *or* **can't** *statement:* *I can't pass this test. I'm too dumb for chemistry.*

Self-compassionate rewrite: *This test might be very difficult, but I will study and do my best.*

1. *Can't* statement: I can't tell myself that I'm good enough. It's a lie.

   Self-compassionate rewrite:

2. *Should* statement: I should lose weight before I try on clothes for the party.

   Self-compassionate rewrite:

3. *Can't* statement: I can't take this test without cheating.

   Self-compassionate rewrite:

4. *Should* statement: I should not have asked them out. I knew they would reject me.

   Self-compassionate rewrite:

5. *Should* statement: I shouldn't need help for my anxiety.

   Self-compassionate rewrite:

6. *Can't* statement: I can't get into any of the colleges I want to go to.

   Self-compassionate rewrite:

Jot down some *can't* and *should* statements that you typically say to yourself and then reframe them using more self-compassionate and realistic language.

1.
2.
3.
4.
5.
6.

DEFUSING FROM THOUGHTS 1

Thoughts have a lot of power over you when you are "fused" (overidentified) with them. You forget they are just happening in your mind and aren't 100 percent true. There are many "defusion techniques" to help unhook you from unkind, painful, or negative thoughts. These techniques strip negative thoughts of their intensity and help you see them more clearly for what they are.

Give each of these defusion techniques below a try. If you're not having any worrying thoughts right now, try to remember how you felt the last time they cropped up.

Leaves on a stream. Close your eyes and imagine that there are leaves flowing past you on a quiet stream. Every time you notice a thought, take it and place it on the leaf and let it float away, with new leaves coming into view, ready for more of your thoughts.

Waves in an ocean. Imagine writing your thought or worry out in the sand and allowing the tide to wash it away. This is a great metaphor for how impermanent your thoughts are and will allow you not to stay with one thought for too long.

Clouds in the sky. Imagine a blue sky with fluffy white clouds slowly drifting by. Your mind is the sky; your thoughts are the clouds. Let your thoughts float through your mind much like clouds in the sky. As the clouds drift past you, imagine one thought resting on each cloud and floating away.

"I am having the thought that . . ." When a thought comes up, say it out load or write it down. For example, "I am having the thought that I won't make any friends in high school." This allows your mind to realize that you are not your thoughts and that thoughts are temporary.

Who's in charge here? Treat your negative or unkind thoughts as a bully and use fun, imaginative language to reestablish your authority over your mind.

Say or sing it silly. Write down a negative belief you have and pick a silly voice to say or sing it in. Do it over and over until you start laughing or until the belief loses a little bit of its power. Try it—it's fun!

View from above. When you're going through difficulties that are flooding you with stressful or negative thoughts, imagine yourself leaving your body and watching the situation from above. Then zoom out and take a look at the physical space you're in (such as your bedroom or the library). Then zoom out farther to see the entire city you're in. Zoom out farther and see your country and then Earth from space. This helps you place yourself and your troubles in the context of the wider world. Gaining this perspective often makes our struggles seem a bit less daunting.

Repeat the thought. Repeat the difficult thought until you can hear what you're saying without your mind giving it meaning. For example, when you say "milk" over and over again, it stops sounding like a word.

After trying some of these exercises, write about one or two that you found helpful and the reasons why.

Next time you're noticing that you're stuck on a thought, you can use this exercise again to mindfully defuse.

DEFUSING FROM THOUGHTS 2

Defusion exercises increase our psychological flexibility. Cultivating a more flexible mind is both an example of mindfulness and a way to make more opportunities to practice self-compassion.

Now that you're getting the hang of defusion techniques, here are some more for you to try out.

Let go with gratitude. Write down any thoughts that are troubling you or weighing you down. Let them blow away with the wind as you acknowledge that they were trying to protect you but that you're ready to let them go.

Be like a palm tree. Palm trees bend and sway in hurricanes without breaking. They are able to withstand some of the most destructive weather and still bounce back to be our shade—tall and beautifully green, sometimes with coconuts to spare! Think of yourself as a palm tree. Even when your thoughts or emotions feel like hurricane winds, know that you can flex with it, without breaking. When the weather clears, you'll be back up in no time, no worse for the wear.

Be like a mountain. Place your feet firmly on the ground and imagine yourself as a mountain and your thoughts as the constantly changing weather. You are firm and unmoving—undeterred by the weather. Sometimes there be will blizzards, and sometimes the skies will be clear and sunny. You will watch the weather all around you as you stand strong.

Your mind as your friend. Imagine that the thoughts you are having are being said by your friend about themselves. How would you respond to them if it was their story they were telling?

Turn down the volume. Imagine that your thoughts are like a constant stream of news on the radio. The on/off button isn't working, but you can lower the volume to make them quieter.

After reading through and practicing some of these exercises, reflect on how they help you create a more self-compassionate inner voice.

IDENTIFYING STRENGTHS

On the days when you're not feeling great about yourself, you can call on the strengths that you know you have and are always present for you.

Place a check mark next to your strengths and underline those that you'd like to develop.

☐ Adaptable	☐ Dedicated	☐ Intelligent	☐ Resourceful
☐ Adventurous	☐ Dependable	☐ Kind	☐ Respectful
☐ Ambitious	☐ Detail-oriented	☐ Lively	☐ Responsible
☐ Analytical	☐ Determined	☐ Logical	☐ Self-assured
☐ Appreciative	☐ Disciplined	☐ Modest	☐ Self-controlled
☐ Artistic	☐ Empathetic	☐ Moral	☐ Serious
☐ Assertive	☐ Energetic	☐ Motivated	☐ Social
☐ Athletic	☐ Enthusiastic	☐ Observant	☐ Spiritual
☐ Authentic	☐ Fair	☐ Open-minded	☐ Spontaneous
☐ Calm	☐ Flexible	☐ Optimistic	☐ Straightforward
☐ Caring	☐ Focused	☐ Organized	☐ Strategic
☐ Charming	☐ Friendly	☐ Original	☐ Strong leader
☐ Clever	☐ Generous	☐ Outgoing	☐ Tactful
☐ Communicative	☐ Good listener	☐ Patient	☐ Team-oriented
☐ Compassionate	☐ Grateful	☐ Peaceful	☐ Thoughtful
☐ Confident	☐ Helpful	☐ Perseverant	☐ Tolerant
☐ Considerate	☐ Honest	☐ Persistent	☐ Trustworthy
☐ Courageous	☐ Humble	☐ Practical	☐ Versatile
☐ Creative	☐ Humorous	☐ Problem-solving	☐ Warm
☐ Curious	☐ Independent	☐ Quick-witted	☐ Welcoming
☐ Decisive	☐ Inquisitive	☐ Resilient	☐ Wise

Pick five of your strengths and write about how each allows you to meet yourself with more self-compassion during difficult situations.

Example: I am energetic. When I'm feeling down or agitated, I can use that energy to spend quality time with friends or even go for a run.

Strength 1:

Strength 2:

Strength 3:

Strength 4:

Strength 5:

Now that you're more familiar with your strengths, you will know which ones to amplify when you aren't feeling good about yourself or are going through a difficult situation and don't know how to deal.

LIVING BY YOUR VALUES TO MOTIVATE YOURSELF

Living by your values is a self-compassionate way of connecting with yourself and others. It also helps you stay motivated and encourages you to develop a greater sense of identity.

Values are very strongly held beliefs that guide the choices you make in your life. They help you shape how to live your life and the kind of person you want to be. If, for example, friendship is something you strongly value, you will make sure to answer your friends' texts and be there for them when they're down.

A focus on values also allows you to keep your mind on the bigger picture when things get stressful and overwhelming. And it can also help release you from any focus on external validation.

Look at the following list of values and determine which you consider very important, important, and not important. Highlight each group in a different color.

Pick no more than 10 very important ones.

☐ Accomplishment	☐ Compassion	☐ Efficiency	☐ Goodwill
☐ Abundance	☐ Competence	☐ Environment	☐ Goodness
☐ Accountability	☐ Concern for others	☐ Equality	☐ Gratitude
☐ Accuracy	☐ Confidence	☐ Excellence	☐ Hard work
☐ Achievement	☐ Connection	☐ Exploration	☐ Harmony
☐ Adventure	☐ Conservation	☐ Fairness	☐ Holistic living
☐ Autonomy	☐ Cooperation	☐ Faith	☐ Honesty
☐ Balance	☐ Coordination	☐ Faithfulness	☐ Honor
☐ Challenge	☐ Creativity	☐ Family	☐ Improvement
☐ Change	☐ Credibility	☐ Flexibility	☐ Independence
☐ Clarity	☐ Decisiveness	☐ Forgiveness	☐ Individuality
☐ Cleanliness/ orderliness	☐ Democracy	☐ Freedom	☐ Initiative
	☐ Determination	☐ Friendship	☐ Inner peace
☐ Collaboration	☐ Discipline	☐ Frugality	☐ Innovation
☐ Commitment	☐ Discovery	☐ Fun	☐ Integrity
☐ Communication	☐ Diversity	☐ Generosity	☐ Intelligence
☐ Community	☐ Education	☐ Genuineness	☐ Joy

Continued >

Living by Your Values to Motivate Yourself *Continued >*

- ☐ Justice
- ☐ Knowledge
- ☐ Leadership
- ☐ Learning
- ☐ Love
- ☐ Loyalty
- ☐ Moderation
- ☐ Modesty
- ☐ Nature
- ☐ Nurturing
- ☐ Obedience

- ☐ Open-mindedness
- ☐ Optimism
- ☐ Patriotism
- ☐ Peace/nonviolence
- ☐ Perseverance
- ☐ Persistence
- ☐ Personal growth
- ☐ Personal health
- ☐ Practicality
- ☐ Preservation
- ☐ Privacy

- ☐ Problem-solving
- ☐ Professionalism
- ☐ Progress
- ☐ Prosperity
- ☐ Punctuality
- ☐ Purpose
- ☐ Straightforwardness
- ☐ Strength
- ☐ Success
- ☐ Teamwork
- ☐ Timeliness

- ☐ Tolerance
- ☐ Tradition
- ☐ Tranquility
- ☐ Trust
- ☐ Truth
- ☐ Unity
- ☐ Vitality
- ☐ Wisdom

Let's Reflect:

Explain why you chose certain values as very important to you.

> *Example: I chose family because my family is really important to me. I always think about how to make them happy, and I love spending time with them.*

In what ways are you not living by your very important values?

> *Example: Lately, I have been saying really mean things to my sibling because I've been in a bad mood.*

How can you use these values to motivate yourself in a more compassionate way?

> ***Example:*** *If I remind myself how important my family is to me, I can make better choices by not taking my anger out on my sibling.*

GRATITUDE IS THE ATTITUDE

Have you ever noticed how good it feels when you genuinely express thanks to someone or reflect on what you're thankful for? Well, it turns out that practicing gratitude is a powerful antidote to stress and negative thinking. Expressing gratitude for yourself or others can also be an excellent way of practicing self-compassion.

FUN FACTS ABOUT GRATITUDE:

* Offering a "thank you" can open a door to new friendships and keep old ones strong.
* Grateful people tend to have better physical and psychological health.
* Gratitude increases empathy and decreases agitation.
* Gratitude reduces your tendency to compare yourself to others, improving self-esteem.
* Gratitude helps you flex important mental muscles that make you more resilient to stress.

Let's look at how we can adopt a grateful attitude.

Write down five things you are thankful for today.

Think of a difficult situation that you've gone through—perhaps something that has caused you to have negative thoughts or painful emotions. Can you find something in that situation to be grateful for?

> **Example:** *My friend always invites himself over to my house but never invites me to his. When I asked him about it, he got really mad at me and told me he'd never come over to my house again. I guess I'm grateful for my courage to ask him what was going on.*

How does your body, mind, and mood change when you choose gratitude as your attitude?

What is one way you can be sure to practice gratitude the next time you're feeling anxious, stressed, or negative?

Example: I will write a thank-you note to one person during my day.

Think of one thing you're grateful for in each category:

Person:

Quality:

Skill:

Interest:

Memory:

Challenge you overcame:

Favorite TV show:

Favorite band or singer:

Favorite hobby:

TIPS:

★ Buy a fun bedside journal in your favorite color or design and dedicate it to daily gratitude. At the end of each day, write down three things you are grateful for from that day. Be specific. When you wake up the next morning, read them over. Some days it can be hard to find something to be thankful for. In those cases, think about a favorite pet, a delicious meal you had, or a favorite song you listened to that day.

★ You will surely face tough times in adolescence. When you go through a difficult experience, see what happens when you say, "I'm grateful for this experience teaching me something important"— even if you don't know what that lesson is yet.

PUTTING IT ALL TOGETHER, MINDFULLY

BEFRIENDING YOURSELF

The things you say (or don't say) to yourself when you're having a difficult time are usually very different from how you talk to your closest friends. When you speak to others, you're probably more supportive, warm, and loving. By recognizing this stark difference, you can start learning how to become your own best friend. If words of encouragement and compassion help ease others' pain, let's see what happens when you turn them around to yourself.

Close your eyes and think about a good friend or someone you care about going through a difficult time. How would you talk to this person?

Now close your eyes and think about a difficult scenario you struggled with. How did or would you talk to yourself?

Reflect on the similarities and differences. Why are there differences?

What might be different if you always spoke to yourself in a self-compassionate way?

Shortcut practice:

When you're struggling, stressed, hurting, or unmotivated, simply ask yourself, "What would I say to my best friend (or favorite pet or family member) if this were them?"

REFRAME WITH SELF-KINDNESS

Have you ever made a mistake or had hurt feelings, and your response was to criticize what you did wrong and to remind yourself of how stupid you were? Did that make you feel better or worse? One of the core practices of self-compassion is replacing judgmental and critical self-talk with kinder statements.

Here are two difficult scenarios, each followed by a critical response and a response reframed with self-kindness. Read them over and then try creating a few scenarios and responses of your own.

Situation: You messed up your lines in a song or play, and it threw off the other person onstage.

Critical voice: I can't believe I did that! I'm such an idiot, and I'm so embarrassed. Everyone saw how badly I messed up. I don't think I could ever show my face onstage again. My director probably hates me.

Self-kindness reframe: Ouch! That was a tough thing to go through. I can now imagine how others feel when they mess up in public. That was a bit embarrassing, but it was only a play. I'll study my lines better and hopefully won't make that mistake again. It's okay to make mistakes, after all.

Situation: You got caught cheating off your friend's exam.

Critical voice: Oh my gosh, my parents are going to kill me. I'm so dumb. I shouldn't have done that. Why didn't I just study more on my own? I'll never be able to make this grade up. I'm such a bad person for cheating.

Self-kindness reframe: I realize I didn't make a great decision, but everyone makes mistakes. I'm going to learn from this experience so that I don't have to go through this again.

Now you try. Write about a few situations you've been in that you responded to with self-criticism.

Situation:

Critical voice:

Self-kindness reframe:

Situation:

Critical voice:

Self-kindness reframe:

Situation:

Critical voice:

Self-kindness reframe:

Situation:

Critical voice:

Self-kindness reframe:

How did self-kindness feel compared to self-criticism?

SELF-COMPASSION BREAK

This exercise is an effective and simple way to incorporate self-compassion into your day.

This series of self-compassionate statements is broken up into three categories (mindfulness activation, common humanity reminders, and self-kindness intentions). When you're having a difficult time, relief can come from simply repeating them. To try them out, think of a situation in your life that is stressful or painful. Bring to mind how it makes you feel, both physically and emotionally. Then choose a statement and say it out loud or to yourself.

Mindfulness Activation

"This hurts."   *"This is a moment of suffering."*
"This is a moment of pain."   *"This is pain."*
"This is hard."   *"This is stressful."*

These statements bring you to a present state of mind by simply acknowledging your current experience.

Common Humanity Reminders

"I'm not alone."   *"Everyone struggles."*
"Other teenagers feel like this."   *"Everyone has stress."*
"Most teens go through this."   *"Everyone has difficult feelings."*
"Everyone gets scared."

These loving-kindness statements remind you that your struggles are ones that teens go through all over the world.

Self-Kindness Intentions

"May I be kind to myself."   *"May I forgive myself."*
"May I feel calm."   *"May I feel relief."*
"May I feel courageous."   *"May I accept myself as I am."*
"May I be free from hurt."

These statements create a feeling of warmth, comfort, and care.

Pick a few of the statements that really speak to you so you can say them out loud or in your mind anytime you need to hear them. A self-compassion break is always deserved!

GIVING YOURSELF WHAT YOU NEED

The magic of self-compassion is that it helps you determine what you need in a moment of suffering. You don't have control over what others do, and you can't go back in time to change mistakes you may have made. But when you are hurting, you can ask yourself, "What do I need?"

This question serves as shorthand for several other questions, which include:

* What do I need to hear?

* What do I need to feel comforted?

* What can I do for myself if I am struggling?

* What might ease or simply acknowledge my hurt?

Here are some common situations that teens experience. Take some time to imagine yourself in each of these difficult scenarios. Write down how you might feel (or have felt) during each experience. Then take a moment to think deeply about what you might need—what you could offer yourself that would give you comfort or help you feel understood.

1. I found out that the person I like doesn't like me back.

   How do I feel?

   What do I need?

2. I just heard that there is an unkind rumor being spread about me.

   How do I feel?

   What do I need?

3. I just got two bad grades on my report card.

How do I feel?

_____

_____

What do I need?

_____

_____

_____

4. I just got grounded by my parents for coming home late.

How do I feel?

_____

_____

What do I need?

_____

_____

Now try to come up with two scenarios in your life (past or present) that could use some self-compassion practice:

Scenario 1:

How do I feel?

_____

_____

What do I need?

_____

_____

_____

Scenario 2:

How do I feel?

What do I need?

This exercise will help you begin to ask the important question, "What do I need?" instead of punishing yourself or engaging in another unhelpful behavior.

LOVING YOUR IMPERFECT SELF

It's easy to feel like you're the only one who isn't smart enough, skinny enough, fit enough, cool enough, or funny enough. Here is your new truth: Every single human on earth—including every single teen, even the ones you see on shiny Instagram—is imperfect.

Think about the word *perfect*. What does it mean to you? How do you define perfection?

Are there others in your life whose definition of perfection you try to live by? Why do you feel you need to live by these definitions?

What are things about you that you see as not _____ enough?

If there were no one else (such as friends or family) influencing your definition of "enoughness," how could you create a more self-compassionate definition for yourself?

Are there more neutral ways to look at your imperfections?

Example: I have acne. It's a skin condition that thousands of teens have.

Are there more positive ways to look at your imperfections?

Example: Having acne made me self-conscious and uncomfortable, so I used self-compassion to focus on things I like about myself instead. If my little brother ever has acne, I can talk to him about how to cope self-compassionately with it.

What are some more self-compassionate ways you can talk to yourself when you're feeling like you aren't good enough or perfect enough?

Take a moment to practice the following statements. Write or say them until doing so feels easy and true for you.

"I accept that I am imperfect."   "I am imperfect and unique."
"I am imperfect, and that's okay."   "I am good enough."
"I accept that I am good enough."

EMBRACING OUR COMMON HUMANITY

Acknowledging our common humanity is an integral part of self-compassion practice because during stressful times, you can feel isolated and alone. It seems like you're the only one going through this kind of struggle. Your brain tells you that nobody but you make mistakes, messes up in friendships, endures heartbreak, or fails exams. Acknowledging our common humanity helps you create connections with others in your mind or in real life, which makes your struggle feel more manageable. Remember that suffering and failing are part of the human experience.

You are not alone! I hope that you can take this very important statement and put it right into your heart.

Next time you feel isolated and alone, you can come back to this exercise to remind yourself that your struggle is truly everyone else's struggle.

This exercise will help you remember that you're sharing a common human experience each time you're struggling with a difficult emotion.

Situation 1:

Pick a situation that has caused you suffering. For example, you lost a friend because he found out you said something unkind about him.

Do you know someone else who has been through this? If not, can you imagine someone your age somewhere in the world going through the same type of thing? Close your eyes and picture everyone who has been through this, holding one another's hands—all connected. How does envisioning this help you feel less alone?

What have you been saying to yourself in this situation that has made you feel more alone or isolated? For example, "I am a really bad friend. I'm the worst friend."

What can you say to remind yourself of your shared human experience? For example, "I made a mistake, as all friends do. It hurts to lose someone, especially when you're the one who hurt them. It's painful to go through this, and I'm sure others have had the same experience. I feel empathy for them, even though—like me—they did something wrong."

Situation 2:

Pick a situation that has caused you suffering.

Have you ever known anyone else who has been through this?

What have you been saying to yourself in this situation that has made you feel more alone or isolated?

What can you say to remind yourself of your shared human experience?

MOTIVATING WITH LOVE

When you try to motivate yourself through fear or self-dislike, positive changes rarely happen. A kinder, more caring approach is usually more successful.

In this exercise, you will challenge yourself to find a more self-compassionate kind of motivation. Think of yourself as a character such as Dumbledore from Harry Potter or a similarly wise, kind soul offering you motivation. What would that sound like?

Jot down three goals, behaviors, or activities that you'd like to motivate yourself to do. For each, write down a fear-based way of motivating yourself, followed by a compassionate approach.

Example:

Goal/behavior/activity: Building a new habit, trying something new, asking someone out, telling your parents about something, doing a homework assignment— anything that requires motivation and self-talk.

Fear motivation: I'm going to go to the gym every day because I'm too fat right now.

Compassionate motivation: I accept my body as it is, but I want to get stronger, and going to the gym will help me do that.

Now you give it a try.

Goal/behavior/activity:

Fear motivation:

Compassionate motivation:

Goal/behavior/activity:

Fear motivation:

Compassionate motivation:

Goal/behavior/activity:

Fear motivation:

Compassionate motivation:

Reflection: Looking over your examples, how does the compassionate motivation make you feel versus the fear motivation? Which one makes it more likely that you will try something you're scared to do?

> **TIP:**
> When we change because we don't like something about ourselves, the changes are often negative or short-lived. When we try to change out of a place of loving and caring for ourselves, wanting to see ourselves thrive, the changes are positive and long-lasting.

GETTING ACTIVE WITH COMPASSIONATE MOVEMENT

Activity can be a form of self-compassion. Moving around and stretching helps us feel physically better, lighter, and less tense. Use compassionate movement when you are really feeling the stress of your day or when you want to bring your attention to your physical self and get out of your busy mind.

Let's Give It a Try

1. Stand up and go to a spot where you will have some space to move around.

2. Spread your legs shoulder-width apart. Feel your feet firmly on the floor. Imagine you are a strong tree or a mountain rooted in the ground. Take a few deep breaths and acknowledge filling your body with air.

3. Sway gently from side to side, feeling your feet and legs working underneath you.

4. Start to explore the different movements you can do with your legs—squatting, bending, walking, lunging, stretching. Really feel your body releasing tension.

5. Move your torso, and stretch it gently in all different directions. Breathe deeply as you do. Open up your chest cavity and let more air into your lungs.

6. Move your arms around, stretching them in ways that feel good. Open and close your hands and fingers.

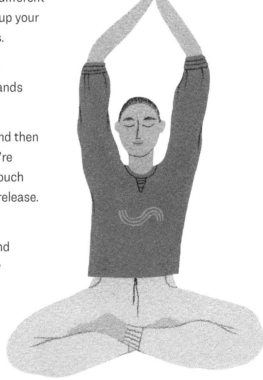

7. Very gently stretch your neck side to side and then roll your shoulders forward and back. If you're comfortable doing so, bend slowly over to touch your toes and feel the tension in your back release. Take a deep breath.

8. As you move your body with compassion and care, occasionally say to yourself, "My body deserves some love and affection."

9. Now take some time to do whatever your body feels it wants to do—sitting, standing, or lying down. Be kind, gentle, comforting, and safe.

How did it feel to take a break and give some attention to your body? What parts of your body really needed it?

In what situations do you think these exercises would be helpful? For example, taking breaks while writing homework.

> TIP:
> Compassionate movement can be anything you want it to be, as long as your intention is to give your body some attention and comfort. For example, a walk through the park, 10 minutes of yoga, or even a workout at the gym.

HAND OVER HEART

When you're feeling fear, discomfort, anger, or pain, your brain activates your nervous system and tells you that there's something threatening you. This is the fight-flight-freeze response or stress response that we discussed earlier in the book.

But your brain can also activate something known as the "care system," which causes positive, calming hormones like oxytocin (also known as the "love" hormone) to flow through your body. One of the things that activates this system is physical touch. This is why babies start to calm down when they are held. This exercise is designed to help you switch your brain from activating a stress response to turning on the care system.

When you recognize the fight-flight-freeze response, practice this simple but powerful exercise. It may feel silly at first, but give it a try.

1. Find a place where you can sit or lie comfortably—or simply do this exercise right where you are.

2. Once you're settled, take a moment to think about what's hurting or worrying you—for example, someone just broke up with you, you failed an exam, or your parents yelled at you.

3. Close your eyes. Take a deep breath in through your nose, filling your belly and lungs. Then breathe out slowly through your mouth.

4. Slowly place your hand over your heart. If you're able to place palm against skin, that can be even more effective.

5. Begin to feel the soft pressure and warmth of your hand pressing against your chest. Feel your chest rise and fall with your breath. Acknowledge how it feels to hold your hand against your heart as you breathe. When your mind wanders, simply remind yourself you're focusing on your hand over your heart.

6. As you continue to breathe and hold your hand over your heart, try saying out loud or internally, "You are hurting, and you are seen" or, "This is painful." Choose a short and simple phrase that notices your pain. Use language that works for you—just make sure it's gentle.

7. You may practice this as long as you wish—30 seconds or 30 minutes. Just remember that this exercise actually activates a natural part of your care system that counteracts the stress response, and this is exactly what we need when we're struggling.

8. Do this anytime, anywhere. Even if you're feeling good.

TIP:

If for any reason holding a hand over your heart is uncomfortable for you, you're more than welcome to place a hand over your belly or even give yourself a soft hug with your hands on your shoulders. Find a gesture that makes you feel safe and offers compassion.

PROGRESSIVE MUSCLE RELAXATION

This is a tried-and-true exercise that allows you to offer compassion and caring attention to your body. If you're feeling anxious, angry, restless, tired, lonely, sad, in physical pain, or irritated, this exercise can help you be more present and calmer in your body. It is also a practice in mindfulness. Paying attention to physical sensations helps you get out of your mind. Instead of being unkind to yourself and dwelling on stressful thinking, lie down on your bed or on a yoga mat and take a break.

1. Lie down somewhere you can be comfortable, such as your bed or a yoga mat.

2. Let your hands fall at your sides, and spread your feet apart.

3. Close your eyes and start taking some deep breaths, in through the nose, out through the mouth. Continue breathing deeply throughout the exercise.

4. When your mind wanders, gently say to yourself, "I'm lying here, focused on my body."

5. Starting at the top of your head, tense only your forehead, perhaps by furrowing your brow or raising your eyebrows. Maintain that tension for five seconds, making sure you are not tensing any other parts of your body. Then release.

6. Now bring your attention to the middle of your face—your nose and your cheeks. Scrunch up your face as tightly as you can for five seconds, feeling the tension. Then release and feel the sensation of comfort.

7. Continue to move down your entire body this way, tensing as many muscle groups as you can for five seconds each and then releasing. Focus on these muscles:

   * Forehead and eyebrows (raise or furrow your eyebrows as much as you can)

   * Cheeks and nose (scrunch your face)

   * Mouth and jaw (open or smile wide for tension)

   * Neck (gently tighten your neck muscles)

   * Shoulders (push them up toward your ears)

* Chest (hold your breath for 10 seconds)

* Abdomen (flex your stomach muscles)

* Upper arms (fold your lower arms in as if you're showing off your upper arm muscles)

* Lower arms (hyperextend your entire arm to create tension)

* Hands (create tight fists)

* Buttocks (clench and release)

* Thighs (lock your thigh muscles by stretching your legs out)

* Calves and shins (tense your calf and shin muscles)

* Ankles (bend your feet upward to create ankle tension)

* Feet (clench all muscles in your feet)

* Toes (point and curl your toes; spread your toes)

* Entire body (tighten and release all your muscles)

After you've finished, take some time to reflect on the exercise. How did you feel before you started? How are you feeling now? Be sure to check in with both body and mind.

TIPS:

1. If you'd like to have a soft voice guide you through these exercises, go on YouTube and search for "guided progressive muscle relaxation." You can also pick one of these to do on the go when you need to release some tension. Clenching your hands into fists and clenching your buttocks are two that can be really helpful on their own.

2. Be sure to be safe and compassionate toward your body. If there is a muscle that's hurting, it may be unsafe to tense. Please listen to your body and move to another muscle.

The main goal of this exercise is to help your mind stay focused on the sensation of tensing (the buildup, the shaking of the muscle, maybe even slight discomfort) and the sensation of releasing (blood flowing back into the muscle, a sense of relaxation). When you tense up, picture all your stress and pain energy going into that muscle group. The slower you go through this exercise, the longer you can spend in a more relaxed state.

MAKING YOUR MANTRA

A mantra is a statement you can say to yourself when you're struggling in a difficult situation.

In this exercise, you will create two mantras—a soothing one to help you feel calmer and more grounded, and a protective one that you can use when you are ready to act in the world with fierce self-compassion.

This is a list of words that you can mix and match to create your mantras, if you wish. It's just here to get you started. You are welcome to go outside of this list or create different versions and tenses of the words on the list. Be creative and have fun. This is all yours!

- ☐ Pleasant
- ☐ Cool
- ☐ Powerful
- ☐ Relax
- ☐ Love
- ☐ Create
- ☐ Happiness
- ☐ Soft
- ☐ Time
- ☐ Hope
- ☐ Peaceful
- ☐ River

- ☐ Lovable
- ☐ Rest
- ☐ Joy
- ☐ Warm
- ☐ Calm
- ☐ Serene
- ☐ Smooth
- ☐ Free
- ☐ Sky
- ☐ Loving
- ☐ Harmony
- ☐ Peace

- ☐ Mountain
- ☐ Light
- ☐ Floating
- ☐ Here
- ☐ Breathe
- ☐ Temporary
- ☐ Air
- ☐ Soothing
- ☐ Grounded
- ☐ Enough
- ☐ Space
- ☐ Strong

- ☐ Ocean
- ☐ Release
- ☐ Deserve
- ☐ Accept
- ☐ Comfort
- ☐ Steady
- ☐ Ease
- ☐ Energy
- ☐ Present
- ☐ Surrender

Examples:

You are enough.
I am free.
I am human.
Let it be.

Feeling calm.
Soothe myself.
I am strong.

Create peace.
Let go.
Breathe in and out.

This will pass.
You are the sky.
Be here now.

Write your mantras here.

Soothing mantra: _____

Protective mantra: _____

Why did you choose the words you did? How do they make you feel when you say them?

How will you use these mantras to help you be more self-compassionate?

TIP:

Consider creating an art project or poster to visually represent your mantra. Hang it on your door, inside your locker, or on your wall. For example, a small collage of your favorite nature photos could represent these mantras: "Steady as a mountain" or "Flowing like a river." Be sure to write the mantra down somewhere you can see it amid all the creativity.

EVERY BODY

As a teen, you might be experiencing a changing body—or maybe your body isn't changing as quickly as everyone else's seems to be. This exercise is a self-compassion practice that will allow you to accept your body as it is, instead of wishing it were different. Remember that when we wish for reality to be anything other than what it is, we suffer.

Write down anything that you don't like about or think is wrong with your body.

Write down how believing these things has impacted your life—your mood, goals, thoughts, etc.

Reflect on why you want to learn to be kinder to and more accepting of your body.

Here are some ways to change your perspective to a more self-compassionate one. Take a few moments to reflect on each set of statements.

* When your mind wanders to something you don't like about your body, shift your focus to appreciate all that your body can do. It takes you from place to place, lets you experience life, and allows you to see, hear, smell, and taste beautiful things. Think about all that your body can do and how cool that is!

* If you're on social media and starting the comparison game, put down your device and remind yourself that you will not allow comparison to make you feel worse about your body. Remember that people show their idealized selves online, which is not reflective of the imperfections they see and believe they have.

What could you otherwise do with all that precious time and energy you are spending worrying about how your body looks in clothes, how it compares to others', how much it weighs, etc.?

Can you look at yourself as a whole person—someone with a mind, talents, wonderful qualities, friendships, a family, a pet, life experiences? How would you feel if each time you were focused on a body part, you could zoom out to look at your entire self instead?

A LETTER TO "LITTLE YOU"

If the little-kid version of you were sitting in front of you right now, you wouldn't speak to them using the language that you often use to speak to yourself. It would certainly hurt their feelings and make them worry, don't you think? This is your opportunity to offer self-compassion to "little you." Doing so can help you recognize that little you and current you both need and deserve the same thing.

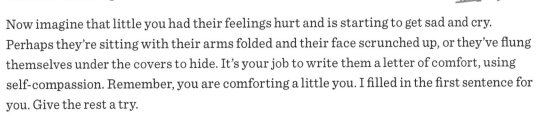

Find a photo of yourself at a younger age—say, around four to six years old. Take some time to look at your cute little self. Really let yourself picture what you were like at that age.

Now imagine that little you had their feelings hurt and is starting to get sad and cry. Perhaps they're sitting with their arms folded and their face scrunched up, or they've flung themselves under the covers to hide. It's your job to write them a letter of comfort, using self-compassion. Remember, you are comforting a little you. I filled in the first sentence for you. Give the rest a try.

Dear little [insert your name],

I want to give you a hug.

_____

_____

_____

Love,

[insert name]

> TIP:
>
> Next time you start to beat yourself up or put yourself down, ask yourself, "Would I say this to a five-year-old me who was struggling and needing comfort?"

THE POWER OF VULNERABILITY

WHAT HAPPENS WHEN PEOPLE OPEN THEIR HEARTS? THEY GET BETTER.

—HARUKI MURAKAMI

The definition of vulnerable is to be exposed to the possibility of being harmed or attacked—either physically or emotionally. While it's natural to try to avoid being vulnerable, when you protect yourself from this exposure, you are likely to use harmful self-talk or behaviors to avoid the discomfort. Having the skill of self-compassion will allow you to be courageous enough to be vulnerable. Vulnerability is a huge strength. It allows you to be open to meaningful experiences in life.

Here are just a few examples of vulnerability. Have you ever been vulnerable in any of the following ways? Place a check mark next to those you've experienced. Feel free to add any others you can think of.

☐ Stood up for yourself

☐ Cried in front of someone

☐ Reached out to a friend in need

☐ Went to a party or dance

- [ ] Raised your hand in class
- [ ] Admitted when you were afraid
- [ ] Said "I love you"
- [ ] Tried out for a play, club, or team
- [ ] Shared your opinion in a group
- [ ] Joined a club with new people
- [ ] Told someone that you were upset
- [ ] Told someone that they hurt you
- [ ] Said no
- [ ] Made a joke that didn't land

- [ ] Spoke in front of the class or a group
- [ ] Introduced yourself to someone new
- [ ] Shared a piece of writing or art with others
- [ ] Said "I like you"
- [ ] Asked for help
- [ ] Shared a difficult story with someone
- [ ] Let yourself feel a difficult emotion in front of another
- [ ] Shared with someone how you felt about them

Chances are, you've checked off quite a few. You should be so proud of yourself—vulnerability is scary!

Write about a recent time when you were vulnerable that didn't go so well. What did it feel like in your body? What were you thinking?

Think about the way you responded to yourself after this incident occurred. Perhaps there was embarrassment, fear, or shame present. Were you kind or punishing to yourself? Were you proud of yourself?

Next time you choose to be vulnerable, and the outcome is uncomfortable, how can you use the principles of self-compassion (self-kindness, common humanity, mindfulness) to make yourself feel better?

TIP:

Any time you catch yourself being courageous enough to be vulnerable, it's a great time to offer yourself some affirmation. You did something so brave—great job!

A LETTER TO YOURSELF—YOUR OWN BEST FRIEND

Self-compassion allows us to be our own best friends. This exercise will allow you to practice that skill.

Think about anything that makes you feel "not good enough," imperfect, or insecure. Allow yourself to notice and feel any emotions that come up. Try not to push them away, and let yourself fully experience them in this moment.

Use this space to write about any feelings and thoughts that you experienced when thinking about this insecurity.

Now imagine that you are writing a letter to yourself from the perspective of an unconditionally loving, understanding, accepting, and compassionate friend. This friend is extremely similar to you in that they share your strengths and weaknesses. They forgive you even if you act in a hurtful way or fail at something or make a mistake. This friend knows everything about you—your failures and successes, your secrets, the little details that make you who you are. As you write from this dear friend's perspective, think about them speaking to you about your insecurities and perceived inadequacies. What would they say to you? How would they say it?

Grab a separate sheet of paper, and let's start writing!

Example:

Dear _____ ,

Thank you for telling me about what you're struggling with. I'm sorry to hear that you're beating yourself up so much. You aren't alone.

Love,

Your Best Friend

Once you've finished writing, put the letter away—maybe for a few hours, maybe for a few days.

When you're ready to pick it up again, read it to yourself with the intention of feeling and hearing this friend's every word. Allow yourself to really feel as though the most loving person has written this for you. Be open to their compassion, allowing it to comfort you. Perhaps read it a second or third time, letting their compassion become the compassion that you have for yourself.

CHAPTER 3

Cultivating Self-Compassion in Real Life

Now that you've made it through the helpful exercises in chapter 2 and are using the strategies you've learned to practice self-kindness, let's go a step further and see how these skills can be applied in real life. This chapter will cover a range of experiences, many of which will sound familiar to you. That's because they are all real-world situations, experienced by teens I have worked with. I hope that reading them will make you feel less alone in your struggles.

You will see that your peers also struggle with self-judgment, self-doubt, insecurity, shame, and negative thoughts and emotions. Like you, they struggle to navigate social, parental, academic, and friendship challenges, all while growing into a new body and feeling pressure from what feels like every side. And, like you, they often feel as though they are alone and incapable of making it through adolescence successfully.

The tips, tools, and advice I offer are aimed at helping these teens strengthen their self-compassion skills. As you read through them, consider how some may mirror the challenges you are facing and how my suggestions could be applied to your situation. My hope is that after seeing how any difficulty can be successfully addressed in a self-compassionate way, you will be even more excited about continuing to cultivate this important life skill.

LUCY'S STORY

Michelle and I were both supposed to pick the same classes for our first year in high school, but then I found out that she picked a completely different schedule. I'm so upset. Now I'm going to be all alone. I'm sure that she picked different classes because she doesn't want to spend so much time with me. How will I make it through the first year of high school on my own?

KATIE'S RESPONSE

Lucy, you must be feeling abandoned, scared, and let down all at once. That's a lot to feel right before you go to a new school. I'm sorry to hear that Michelle didn't follow through on your plans together. That must have been difficult for you to find out. It sounds like your mind is jumping to the conclusion that she's making this decision purposefully against you, and it also seems that you feel convinced you will be alone through the entire year of high school.

Let's find a different way to respond that will make you feel a little better. Instead of allowing your mind to jump to negative possibilities, take a moment and say to yourself, "Wow, it doesn't feel very good to have a friend break a promise to me." Really mean it as you offer yourself that comfort. An act of protective self-compassion might be to talk to Michelle and ask her directly why she chose different classes. You can be courageous and let her know that it hurt your feelings that she didn't follow through. Instead of focusing your attention on this one event, can you write down five other ways that you might be able to make friends the first year? Try reminding yourself that just because you aren't in class together doesn't mean you're losing your friend altogether. Find a more self-compassionate way to address your fear of being alone. Can you imagine how many kids your age are also afraid that they'll be left without anyone to hang out with? You aren't alone!

SHAWN'S STORY

Pete, Rachel, and I are always hanging out together. I found out that he and Rachel have been spending time alone. I even heard that someone saw them holding hands. He knew I had a crush on her. Of course she picked him. He's taller and more popular than I am. I'm sure she wouldn't have gone out with me even if she knew I liked her. I'm feeling so many things—jealous, betrayed, and left out. How can I possibly keep being friends with them? How can I handle so many feelings at once?

KATIE'S RESPONSE

Shawn, oh, that's so hard. There's that double whammy of feeling betrayed by one best friend and feeling rejected by another. I can only imagine how many thoughts and feelings are coming at you right now. But here's the thing. While I understand you're going through a pretty difficult time right now, I'm not sure that putting yourself down is your best bet at feeling better. What do you think?

Can you say three kind things to yourself about this situation? Perhaps one of them could be that you're a really terrific friend for trying to be happy for them even while you're hurting. I know you don't want to lose either of their friendships. Are you able to practice accepting the situation for what it is? "I accept that Pete and Rachel are together. I accept that I am not with Rachel." Remember, you don't have to like that this is happening, but accepting the truth of the present moment can at least help you tap into some mindful self-compassion. As for the amount of feelings you're experiencing, remember how an emotion really lasts about 90 seconds in the body? Imagine your body is cycling through these emotions. Can you decide how many cycles of each emotion you'd like to go through and time each one? Sit with each emotion separately by labeling them one at a time and noticing what each is like in your body. You'll soon see that you can handle quite a lot and that these difficult emotions won't last forever.

SKYLER'S STORY

I'm a junior, and I wanted to go out to a diner with my friend Graham, who's a senior. He just got an awesome car, but my parents said they don't feel comfortable with me being driven by a 17-year-old. They started asking me all these questions about him, and I started screaming at them, so they grounded me. I'm so pissed off. What's the big deal? Now I don't know if Graham will ever ask me to hang out again.

KATIE'S RESPONSE

It makes a lot of sense why you feel angry at your parents, Skyler. You were being up front by telling them what you wanted to do and where you wanted to go, and you probably feel like they don't trust you. That can be so frustrating when you haven't done anything to show them that you can't handle this kind of situation.

It sounds like the anger seems to be taking over. Can you take a moment and close your eyes to feel it in your body? Before you make an impulsive decision that might get you into more trouble, let's see if we can offer this difficult emotion some room to tire itself out. Is there a heat or pressure you're feeling? Stay with the emotion, even when your mind starts to wander to all the ways you'll get your parents back for this. Let's take five minutes to do some deep breathing like you learned, focusing on a cooling breath going in and a hot, angry breath leaving your body. This will help you stay present without fueling more anger. Then we can come back and see if you're still feeling full of rage. You can also give yourself some words of support. Remind yourself that this realistically won't be the last time you get to go somewhere with an older friend. In fact, soon enough, you'll be the one getting your license. Practice some mindfulness by zooming out from this situation and watching it from above. Is it worth getting this upset about?

ROBIN'S STORY

There are tryouts for the high school soccer team coming up, but I'm too afraid to get out there. My dad keeps telling me I need to do it because he was a soccer player when he was growing up. I do love to play, but there's so much pressure, and I know I'm going to mess up if I go. What if I try and I don't make it?

KATIE'S RESPONSE

I remember how stressful volleyball tryouts were when I was leaving middle school. I hear you, Robin. You must also be feeling so much pressure from your dad. It sounds like you really want to make him happy and proud of you. What is making you so convinced that you'll mess up?

Let's try this. Why don't you tell me what you would say if this were your best friend talking? Would you tell him that he would mess up and that his dad would never forgive him if he didn't go? How might you respond to him if he were so afraid to try and fail? You'd probably tell him that it would be courageous of him to give it a shot, and if he didn't make it, he could always try again the following year or go out for a different sport or team that he really liked. Now let's offer those encouraging words back to yourself. How does it feel to hear yourself say that it will be okay if you don't make the team? I know that you're hearing your dad's voice and your inner monologue telling you all kinds of things. I also know that you do want to make the soccer team because you love the sport. Try imagining that you have a knob to turn the volume down on all those extraneous voices distracting you from being your own best friend at the tryouts. Do you feel that you could try your very hardest if the volume were at a 3 instead of a 15? Instead of letting your thoughts spiral and catastrophizing things, remember that you have control over the volume knob whenever you need it. Who needs that inner critic playing so loud? You've got this!

RILEY'S STORY

Since Campbell broke up with me, I'm always sad. No matter what someone says to me, no matter what funny TV show is on, I can't seem to feel better. I know I'm pushing my friends away, and I feel like I might as well. I'm sure they think of me as such a downer. I don't want to be this sad, but maybe there's just something really wrong with me. That's probably why Campbell broke up with me.

KATIE'S RESPONSE

Oh, Riley, breakups are always so difficult, and I'm sorry to hear that it has been making you so sad. It sounds like you've been replaying all the ways in which this relationship could have gone differently. There is nothing wrong with you, Riley. You're having a normal reaction to someone you really cared about ending their relationship with you. You've said it makes you feel worthless and unwanted.

Let's take a moment. Can you ask yourself, "What do I need in order to comfort myself right now?" I bet the answer isn't "beating myself up and convincing myself that I'm fundamentally flawed." What answers come up for you when you ask what you need in order to feel more at ease and less sad? You mentioned that you need to hear that you are worthy of love and affection and to be reminded that this is just one relationship. Are you able to offer that to yourself? Can you say those things to yourself much like a loving friend would say them to you? It sounds like part of the sadness is being fueled by these thought loops you're getting stuck in. Take some time each day to practice the "leaves on a stream" exercise. Put each thought on a leaf and let it float on by without getting stuck on it. See what happens after a week of giving your mind a break from all those negative thoughts. You won't feel sad forever—remember that emotions are not permanent. A hand on your heart and some kinder words to yourself might help you feel up to seeing your friends. I bet they just want to help support you through this tough time. It sounds like being with others would help you feel less alone right now.

OLIVIA'S STORY

I'm a sophomore in high school, and I haven't had my first kiss yet. I am so behind everyone else. Two of my friends have boyfriends, and they are always talking about how they've gotten past first base. I don't think I can get anyone to like me. I'm so afraid that people are going to think I'm a prude. Maybe I should just go to a party and get drunk so that I can be brave enough to go up to someone and kiss them.

KATIE'S RESPONSE

I know how difficult it is to feel like you're behind in all those important high school milestones. I can see that you're playing that infamous comparison game. I'm sorry that you're bearing the pain of feeling left out. It's such an uncomfortable state to be in—wishing that you could just be like everyone else in the ways you're "supposed" to be, right?

I know that you can catch yourself in that storytelling mode. Let's label it the objective truth: You haven't kissed someone. Your friends have kissed someone. Now let's just notice the story you're telling yourself—that you're not likable, that you're behind everyone, that you need to do something impulsive in order to catch up. This story is making you feel so bad about yourself. Take a moment here to pause and say, "Oh! That's a story." You've told me before that you don't want to kiss someone until you really like them. That is so awesome, Olivia. Offer yourself some affirmation and gratitude for being thoughtful enough to respect your readiness. That's really hard to do, with so much peer pressure around. You can also take a beat and just comfort yourself for how crummy it is to feel left behind. That deserves its own compassionate touch or saying. Let's take a step back and see the situation from an eagle-eye perspective. Is it more likely that you haven't kissed anyone because it simply hasn't been the right time or the right person? The evidence tells you that you have been liked before; you just haven't liked those people back. When you're getting caught up in that negative, self-critical thought stream, remember that you can zoom out, take a step back, and see your situation with more per-spective. It always makes you feel better. Don't you worry. You'll kiss someone someday soon, when the time is right.

KYLAR'S STORY

I can't handle how much my boyfriend and I have been fighting. He often yells at me about what I need to do about all my "mental issues," as he calls them. He knows that I struggle with depression and anxiety, but sometimes he gets fed up with me. When I come home after a bad fight, I go straight into my room. The only thing that makes me feel better is to take a small razor and cut my thigh. I know it's bad, but I just feel such intense pain, and I don't know how else to release it. Sometimes I think about breaking up with him, but it feels too hard.

KATIE'S RESPONSE

Kylar, it's hard to hear that you've been harming yourself. That must mean you're experiencing a brutal amount of pain. I know how sometimes our minds get too loud, our thoughts and feelings are too overwhelming, and it feels like there's nowhere to put that energy. I understand that you choose to cut in order to feel a sense of control over those difficult emotions. Your boyfriend's behavior toward you is really hurtful, and you just want anything to escape the difficult headspace that you're in. I also know that you have wanted to find ways to cope that aren't harmful.

Let's think about the mindfulness practice of "urge surfing." Try to imagine how you were feeling in that moment when you just wanted the pain to become physical instead of emotional. Picture that emotional pain as if it were the thrashing sea, and you are steadily surfing over every big and small wave. Imagine that when a big wave of sadness and anger comes at you, you're strong and confident, surfing that wave instead of fighting against it or wishing it weren't coming for you. You always remain above that sea, but you keep surfing the urges to self-harm until the waves get a little quieter. You know that when you let that urge pass, you always feel a little better, and you can't even remember why you felt so strongly about hurting yourself in the first place. Put a hand on your heart and say that mantra you came up with: "I am safe. I am strong." Repeat it to yourself as you take some deep breaths. When your mind wanders, and you can hear the echo of your boyfriend's comments, say the mantra a little louder and really feel the warmth of your palm against your chest. I know it feels awful in the moment, but allow the moment to pass.

Once you are more self-compassionate, you will see that your boyfriend is not supporting you during a difficult time. Empower yourself with this knowledge. Remember that ending a relationship with someone who doesn't respect or validate your struggle with depression and anxiety is a sign of strength. You deserve to feel validated and understood.

CHARLIE'S STORY

I'm so stupid. A complete idiot. I studied for the exam for hours and even got help from a tutor, but I just kept getting distracted. My whole life, I have had so much trouble paying attention. It sucks. I hate the way my brain works. It makes me too stupid to pass any test or get a good grade. I shouldn't even try, right?

KATIE'S RESPONSE

Charlie, I hear how hard you're being on yourself, and it hurts my heart to hear you call yourself those names. Remember, this is the inner bully's voice. Let's remember what we said we would do when they were giving you grief. Is that voice really all that motivating? Are you really going to buy what it's saying?

Let's practice motivating with compassion and love, not negativity and self-judgment. Remind yourself that you've always had difficulty with attention—that's your brain, not a fundamental flaw of yours. Can you acknowledge how hard it must be for you and your brain to have to expend so much energy when it's so difficult for it to do so? Picture giving your tired brain a hug.

First, remind yourself that the reason you study so hard and get help from tutors is that you value doing well in school. Say to yourself, "I am not stupid at all. I just have difficulty focusing sometimes." Be curious. What are some ways in which you can help yourself focus better during exams? Have you spoken to your teacher about your attentional difficulties? Maybe she has some ideas. That would be a very active self-compassionate thing to try. Now try telling yourself that you know you can pass the next exam. You're going to try each time, and even if you fail, you'll try again. I know it's important for you to meet this challenge—and that's not the voice of an "idiot."

I also know an exercise you love. Let's have you repeat "I am stupid" in the British accent you've been practicing for the play. Don't stop until it's pure gibberish and has us both laughing!

FRANKIE'S STORY

I can't stop scrolling through Instagram even though it's making me feel worse about myself and my life. I follow some celebrities, and I wish I had their life. They have so many friends and so much money. They're so beautiful. Sometimes I spend hours scrolling and thinking about how much of a loser I am compared to them. To make matters worse, I see kids from school posting stories, all hanging out together, but I rarely get invited anywhere. I always have to text them first. It makes me feel lonely and insecure.

KATIE'S RESPONSE

Frankie, social media really makes things difficult for teens, doesn't it? There is just so much content, and it can feel impossible not to compare your life to what you see there. Remember when we spoke about how self-compassion comes in many forms? One of those forms is a more active way of protecting yourself. This might mean that deleting the app from your phone for a few days would be a compassionate choice to make, since it's bringing you down so much.

The story you're telling yourself is that what you see on Instagram is an accurate representation of reality. You're also having the thoughts that you are a loser. On top of that, you see videos of friends hanging out together, and you tell yourself that they are rejecting you because there is something wrong with you. See what I did there? Let's have you practice using a degree of separation between you and what's going on in your mind. Maybe you can practice some curiosity instead of judgment. What do you think your mind is telling you with all these criticisms of comparison? Perhaps it is telling you that you do not feel that you are worthy as you are and that you need to have money and extravagance in order to feel whole. Can you offer yourself a statement of loving-kindness for this? For example, "May I feel worthy." Let's motivate with some compassion now. You are hurting from this behavior of scrolling for hours at a time. What can you plan to do next time you find yourself wanting to mindlessly wander through Instagram? Pick something that you find a lot of joy in so that you feel naturally motivated to do it.

OAKLEY'S STORY

I'm different from most people in my grade. Maybe even in my entire school. I've known for a few years now that I like boys. I could never tell anyone because I would be bullied mercilessly. I've noticed one other gay guy in sophomore year, and I've seen how people treat him, and I would never want that. I feel like I'm hiding who I am from everyone, but I'm also too terrified to tell anyone the truth. I feel desperately alone.

KATIE'S RESPONSE

Oakley, it must be incredibly painful to have to hide who you are. I know how difficult it is to stand out when everything is telling you that you need to fit in.

Let's try the "what do I need" exercise and think about ways to practice self-compassion that will alleviate your feelings of isolation and fear. Here are some examples:

"To soothe myself, I will practice hand-over-heart exercises every night before I go to sleep so that I can shift my attention from difficult thoughts of isolation to those of warmth and care."

"To comfort myself, I will spend more time writing in my journal whenever I'm feeling overwhelmed or sad."

"To validate myself, I will remind myself that other teens who feel they cannot be honest about who they are likely feel very lonely and ashamed. I will be kind and accepting of my pain and not beat myself up for how I've reacted with fear."

"To protect myself, I will stand up for myself if I ever do decide to tell people that I am gay. I will remind myself and anyone who tries to be unkind to me that I know and like who I am, even if I am different. I will make sure to enlist the help of my teachers and counselors so that I can feel supported."

"To support myself, I will look for LGBTQ adolescent groups where I can really know that I belong. What I really need right now is a sense of community. Although I am not getting that at school, I know that there are other ways to meet that important need."

"To motivate myself, I will remember that I deserve to be happy and to be exactly who I am. I will also remember that this situation is not permanent. Sometime in the near future, I will find myself friendships and community that will make me feel accepted. First, I will motivate myself by accepting myself exactly as I am."

FINLEY'S STORY

I haven't gone to school for the last three days. My parents aren't even angry; they just want me to feel better. I feel useless— I can't even push through feeling sad for a few days. The homework was piling up, and I couldn't handle it. I can't handle anything. It's only freshman year, and I know it's only going to get harder from here. It feels like anything that I try, I fail at. Now I can't even get out of bed. I can't do basic life things. Do you really think I could possibly catch up?

KATIE'S RESPONSE

Finley, I'm sorry to hear that you are struggling so much, and on top of that, you are blaming yourself and speaking to yourself so harshly. First, I want to validate that you are struggling with depression. Can you please take a moment and validate the part of you that is really hurting? I know that you think you "should" just be able to handle things, but it's important to know that it is not your fault that your brain is giving you a tough time. This is a great moment to practice some of the self-kindness phrases that you wrote down. "I'm not a failure; I'm just going through a difficult time." "I will feel better and get to enjoy my life again." "I am doing the best that I can right now."

Of course you can catch up! You will catch up. However, it will be much more effective to motivate yourself out of a place of love rather than out of fear. Try saying this to yourself instead: "I am suffering from depression, and it makes it really hard for me to do a lot of everyday things. However, I'm doing what I can to feel better because I really want to be in school with all of my friends. I deserve to feel better, and I'll take it a day at a time."

I know you always talk about how your depression makes you feel like you're the only one who is failing. We spoke about how important it is to remember that you aren't alone. I know it might be hard to imagine, but there are so many teens who are trying to overcome the same challenges you are. Remember how helpful it was for you to close your eyes and picture all the teens who struggle with depression standing side by side, holding hands. Try to hold that powerful image in your mind when you're feeling alone.

HALSEY'S STORY

I'm so upset. There has been a rumor going around about me that I sent naked pictures to this boy at the high school. A few people on Instagram blocked me, and I'm sure that's why. I got mean messages calling me a "slut." Now everyone will think of me like that forever. I feel awful about myself, and it wasn't even true. I was just texting my friend's brother. This makes me feel worthless. What if this rumor gets carried into high school? What should I do to get through this?

KATIE'S RESPONSE

Halsey, that's an incredibly stressful thing to go through. It's awful to hear that 13-year-olds can be this vicious. It must feel so painful to have people saying these things about you. Before we get into problem-solving mode, let's remember how important it is for you to validate how difficult this experience is.

Now is a good time to write down some self-kindness phrases that you can read any time you feel hurt by this situation.

"I am a good and worthy person, and this rumor doesn't define me."

"I deserve to feel safe among my peers."

"I'm going to give myself the support that I need during this difficult time."

"I know I am strong and courageous enough to get through this."

"I know my truth and what happened, and that's what's most important."

How would you be there for your best friend if this were happening to her? You would tell her that you understand she's going through a painful time, and you would give her a lot of words of kindness. You would tell her that you are there for her, and you'd probably try to make her laugh. You might tell her that this rumor will fizzle out and won't carry on forever. Notice how if she were the one struggling, it would be an easy decision for you to give her comfort and loving-kindness. You would remind her that you love and value her despite the rumor. The goal is to treat yourself in this same way when you are the one hurting.

WILLIAM'S STORY

I thought eighth grade was going to be so good, but this summer, my best friend, Ryan, started hanging out with me less and less. When the year started, he was suddenly hanging around the jocks and didn't even say hi to me at lunch. I'm pretty sure I even saw them looking over at me and laughing the other day. I don't understand what I did. He probably doesn't think that I'm cool because I'm a band geek, and he's getting into sports now. I'm really sad about not having him to hang out with, and I've been really lonely. I doubt I'll ever make another close friend again.

KATIE'S RESPONSE

Will, I'm sorry to hear that your best friend hasn't been treating you very well. It must be really difficult to be in your last year of middle school and experiencing a change in one of your most important friendships. This is a good moment to try some mindfulness practice.

Instead of fueling your sadness with self-criticism and catastrophizing, can you ask yourself some questions from a place of curiosity?

"What thoughts am I having that are making these fears bigger?"

"What story am I telling myself about this situation?"

"What else might be going on for Ryan that he is pulling away from our friendship?"

"Are the thoughts I'm having about this situation all 100 percent true and factual?"

"What can I focus on instead so that I can be less upset about this situation?"

Let's also practice some radical acceptance. Remember, it doesn't mean you have to like what's going on, but you can write down some acceptance statements to acknowledge this situation as it is. I know you wish it weren't this way, but for now, it is what's present and true. Take a deep breath between each statement. Say them in a calm yet confident way.

"I accept that Ryan has been spending less time with me and more time with new friends."

"I accept that Ryan has different interests than me."

"I accept that I cannot change his behavior toward me."

How do you feel after you've practiced these acceptance statements? It feels much lighter—even if for a moment—to let go of the weight of a difficult situation by realizing that you cannot change it.

LIAM'S STORY

I get either made fun of or ignored completely at school. I'm lanky and awkward, and I don't really have the clothes that others have, so most people think I'm a loser. I pretty much just go to school and quietly do my work. I don't talk to anyone, and the only time someone addresses me is to call me a name under their breath. I guess I can't blame them. I know I'm the "weird kid." There is one girl who has been really nice to me, but every time she starts to talk to me, I get really nervous. Do you think she'll realize how weird I am and stop being nice to me, too?

KATIE'S RESPONSE

Liam, I'm so sorry to hear that you are treated that way. Some people can be so cruel. When they struggle with their own insecurities, putting other people down is the way that they can feel more confident about themselves. It's unfair and unkind, but it can be helpful to remind yourself that anyone who goes out of their way to hurt you is only trying to avoid their own feelings of discomfort. Even if you have some quirks about you, it doesn't mean that you deserve to be treated this way. This is an important opportunity to practice self-compassion.

It is difficult to feel so alone. It sounds like this girl is a kind person and hoping to connect with you. Let's work with your worry a little bit. You are worried that she will stop being nice to you once she gets to know you, right? Can you do something about this potential outcome? Let's think about what is and isn't within your control. This will help you know how to compassionately combat self-doubt.

Within your control:
• Your behavior toward this potential friend.
• The story you tell yourself about her.

Out of your control:
• What might happen in the future.
• Her thoughts and behaviors.

Let's think of three encouraging statements you can call to mind when she starts talking to you next time. Remember that supporting yourself in this moment is one thing that you can control. These statements will help you feel more confident to be yourself and engage with this girl.

"I am not just the weird kid. I am really great at school, I draw in my spare time, and I'm a great big brother."

"It would be really great to try to make a friend. Even if it's just in the classroom."

"When she gets to know me a little bit, she might get to see what others have been missing out on."

MILLY'S STORY

I can't believe that I let myself eat fries at lunch today. I'm so fat compared to my friends. They all wear size-zero jeans, and I'm a six. Whenever they want to go shopping, I make up an excuse. Lately I've been making sure to count calories and to remember everything I'm eating, but it's exhausting. I should just give up all snack food. I shouldn't be having this much trouble keeping myself from eating. My friend Sam makes it look so easy. How can I possibly be okay with my body when my friends are skinnier than me?

KATIE'S RESPONSE

Milly, I'm sorry to hear how much of a difficult time your mind is giving you about food and your body. Can you please take a moment to hear what your mind is telling you? You're telling yourself that you should be able to keep yourself from nourishing your mind and body with food. Can you close your eyes for a moment and imagine yourself as a little girl? A girl who just wants to be loved and accepted, and a girl who is asking you if she can eat. How would you feel if you were to tell her that she couldn't eat or that she shouldn't eat? Would you tell her that she wasn't as skinny as her friends and therefore wasn't nearly as worthy? I know that it is unimaginable for you to say that to a little girl. So why is it okay for you to say it to yourself?

Let's take a moment to get out of this mindset—even temporarily. It is not about the food, or the weight, or shape of your body. It is something deeper and bigger than that. What is it that you really need to hear in order to feel okay? Do you need to hear that you are acceptable and lovable just as you are? Take a moment to practice saying that to yourself. "I am lovable." "I belong." "I am okay just as I am."

Can you name five things that tell me something about who you are? Can you name three more? Tell me how your weight or your jean size says something about you as a person or about your worth. Do you see how it doesn't actually give us any important information? Instead, close your eyes and picture those words flashing behind your eyelids: "I am too fat." "I am unworthy." "I am ugly." "No one will want me." Acknowledge that those are thoughts, not facts. You don't have to believe them. In fact, believing them hurts you. I know that it feels uncomfortable, but say to yourself, "My body is imperfect, and that is okay." "My body is beautiful as it is because it is mine." "My body does so much for me." Keep repeating these statements. Even if you don't believe them at first, a lot of repetition will help your mind catch on. If you are treating your mind and body with such harshness, then what they need is a lot of warmth and compassion, not starvation.

AUSTEN'S STORY

I have really horrible anxiety in social situations. When I am in a group, my thoughts start racing, and all I can think about is how awkward I must be. I worry about what I'm going to say, and it comes out in a stutter or not at all. I overthink every movement, and I'm constantly fearful that people don't actually want to talk to me, they're just faking it. When I go home, I'll stay up really late wondering what I could have done differently or beating myself up for being such a freak.

KATIE'S RESPONSE

Austen, it sounds like you spend a lot of time in a state of anxiety and worry about what others are thinking about you. That must be so tiring, and it seems as though all the nervousness gets in the way of you feeling comfortable when you are around others. There are three awesome opportunities for self-compassion here—before, during, and after a social interaction.

Right now, when you learn that a group situation is coming up, you probably find yourself remembering the last time that a group interaction didn't go very smoothly, or you think about all the ways in which you're going to mess up. I think we can agree that neither approach is very helpful. A kinder way to offer support to yourself is to say something like, "I've been in groups of people before, and sometimes it's difficult, and other times it is a bit easier. It will be okay, even if I'm not my best self. At least I'm being vulnerable in a situation that's difficult for me. I will go into it with a positive mindset and have a plan for what to do if I get nervous."

During the interaction itself, do your best to focus on listening to what others are saying. This can help you shift your focus away from what you're saying or how you're coming off. When you find yourself getting nervous, quietly take a deep breath, slow down, and tell yourself that you're doing just fine.

After the event, give yourself some positive feedback, even if you believe it didn't go very well. Remind yourself that you didn't have to be perfect, you just had to try—and that there is always an opportunity to be more yourself next time around.

DYLAN'S STORY

I've been in a relationship with Taylor for four months now. At first, things started off really great. I felt so surprised that she would ever go for someone like me. I didn't text her back right away one time, and she sent me paragraphs of texts telling me that I was a terrible girlfriend. I have always had really low self-esteem, and it has been getting worse in this relationship. I feel afraid nearly all the time because it feels like nothing I do will ever be good enough for her.

KATIE'S RESPONSE

Dylan, I'm sorry to hear that you have been feeling this way about yourself in the relationship. Relationships are really hard, especially your first one. It sounds as though some fierce self-compassion is in order.

A partner should be making you feel good and loved in a relationship, not belittled and small.

Can you say aloud the following empowering statements?

"I deserve to be respected in my relationship."

"I deserve to feel good about myself in my relationship."

"I am allowed to speak my mind and advocate for myself in my relationship."

"I deserve to feel safe in my relationship."

How does saying these make you feel? Advocating for yourself in the relationship is a form of fierce self-compassion. You are allowed to tell your girlfriend how you feel, especially if her behavior is hurting you. You might also practice some statements that support your worth. When we believe we are worthy, we are less likely to accept bad treatment from someone else.

"I am worthy of love."

"I am good enough."

"I am lovable."

BRIGHTON'S STORY

I'm first chair in band, vice president of the student council, I volunteer at a retirement home, have a part-time job at a grocery store, I'm taking four APs in my sophomore year, and I am on the varsity tennis team. I'm also studying for the SATs. I have to keep my 4.0 GPA, but I'm in danger of getting a B+ in my chem class, and I'm completely freaking out. I have to do everything perfectly so that I'm set up for my senior year before college. Some days, I wish I could just give everything up and get to relax, but I can't. I have to be perfect, or else I'll disappoint everyone.

KATIE'S RESPONSE

Wow, Brighton—you're doing so much. I'm so impressed, and I hope that you can be proud of yourself. I can completely understand why your anxiety has kicked up a notch, given how overwhelmed and busy you are. It sounds like the core belief "I have to be perfect" is really feeding your fears. Let's practice some self-compassion by replacing this core belief with a few more realistic and mindful ones.

Try repeating these phrases to yourself until they feel truer for you:

"I have already worked so hard to get to where I am. Getting a B+ will not realistically impact my grade, and it is also not helpful for me to negate everything I've done with one less-than-perfect grade."

"Although I have spent a long time believing I needed to be perfect, I know that no one actually is. Setting such expectations for myself only hurts me because I leave no room for error. I can be more forgiving of myself."

"I deserve to relax and take it easy once in a while. I am not performing for other people but rather focusing on the kind of success that I want to have. This means that if others are disappointed, that is not my responsibility. It is okay to let go once in a while."

Remember, there is always a kinder way to respond to yourself. If you had a close friend who had this much on their plate, think about how you might respond to their fear of not being perfect.

CHAPTER 4

Putting Self-Compassion into Action

In this section, you will have an opportunity to put those self-compassion skills you've been working on into action and further experience the benefits of journaling. It can be incredibly helpful in sorting out your thoughts and emotions and framing things in a more self-compassionate way.

The following 10 prompts deal with difficult feelings or situations that teens often experience. On the first page of each, follow the prompt, including what your inner critic was saying in your head and the feelings that surfaced. On the next page, put self-compassion into action and respond with compassionate, reassuring, kind, and positive words. Think about how you would speak to a friend coming to you with this same challenge—and act like your own best friend!

Name one thing about your body that makes you feel inadequate. Explain in detail your thoughts and feelings of insecurity about it and how you think they have affected you. On the next page, put self-compassion into action.

Voice of self-compassion:

Describe a time when you felt like you really messed up in school and how you may have criticized yourself and beat yourself up about it emotionally. What was the outcome? On the next page, put self-compassion into action.

Voice of self-compassion:

Write about a time when you felt really rejected by someone. Elaborate on what happened and how you felt and spoke to yourself afterward. On the next page, put self-compassion into action.

Voice of self-compassion:

Think of a time when you didn't feel as though you belonged or fit in. Write in detail about the difficult emotions and negative thinking that happened as a result. On the next page, put self-compassion into action.

Voice of self-compassion:

Describe one experience on social media that made you feel bad or where you got caught up in comparing yourself. What did your inner critic say? On the next page, put self-compassion into action.

Voice of self-compassion:

Think of an experience when you felt pressure or expectations from an important adult in your life. Explore in detail how this pressure made you feel and think. On the next page, put self-compassion into action.

Voice of self-compassion:

Write about an experience of deep self-doubt or a time when you didn't believe in yourself. What were the negative thoughts that continued the cycle of insecurity? On the next page, put self-compassion into action.

Voice of self-compassion:

Describe a difficult experience you had in a friendship that left you and your friend both hurting. What were some critical and judgmental ways you responded to the struggle? On the next page, put self-compassion into action.

Voice of self-compassion:

Reflect on a time when you felt shame. How did it make you feel? In which unhelpful or negative ways did you continue to water the seeds of shame? On the next page, put self-compassion into action.

Voice of self-compassion:

Name one core belief that negatively impacts part of your life. Describe how you believe it was formed and the unhealthy ways it affects you. On the next page, put self-compassion into action.

Voice of self-compassion:

Next Stop: A Kinder, Gentler, Happier You

Congratulations! You've made it through the workbook. I'm so proud of you, and you should be very proud of yourself.

Take a moment to reflect on the progress you've made. Notice how comforting it feels to have a self-compassionate response ready to go at any moment. Don't worry if you sometimes struggle putting your new skills into play—learning new skills is never a straight path. Know that some days it will feel easier than others to be kind to yourself. It's a practice that needs positive reinforcement, affectionate attention, commitment, and consistency.

I really encourage you to keep a journal where you can write down anything you're feeling bad about, record what your critical voice is telling you, and then reframe the negativity with self-compassion.

As you begin putting self-compassion into action in your daily life, continue to ask yourself two very important questions: "How would I talk to my best friend about this?" and "What do I need right now in order to feel better?"

With your new self-compassionate voice, I know you will navigate this period of self-discovery with less stress and more ease. Your ability to practice mindfulness and self-kindness will transform the way that you experience challenges. Remember, you will always have this handy workbook to look back on when you want to refresh a skill or need a reminder. I promise that in a few years, you will remember this time and be incredibly proud of having developed such a meaningful way to cope with life's struggles. Now it's time to give yourself some positive encouragement and praise for your hard work. You did it!

Resources

RESOURCES FOR TEENS

BOOKS

Be Mindful Card Deck for Teens by Gina M. Biegel, 2016.

Be You Card Deck for Teens: 60 Mindfulness Practices to Manage Anxiety, Build Confidence and Be the True You by Brian Leaf and Matt Oestreicher, 2019.

Chicken Soup for the Teenage Soul: Stories of Life, Love and Learning by Jack Canfield, Mark Victor Hansen, and Kimberly Kirberger, 1997.

Conquer Anxiety Workbook for Teens: Find Peace from Worry, Panic, Fear, and Phobias by Tabatha Chansard, 2019.

Just as You Are: A Teen's Guide to Self-Acceptance and Lasting Self-Esteem by Michelle Skeen and Kelly Skeen, 2018.

Mindfulness for Teens in 10 Minutes a Day: Exercises to Feel Calm, Stay Focused & Be Your Best Self by Jennie Marie Battistin, 2019.

The Mindfulness Journal for Teens: Prompts and Practices to Help You Stay Cool, Calm, and Present by Jennie Marie Battistin, 2019.

Stuff That Sucks: A Teen's Guide to Accepting What You Can't Change and Committing to What You Can by Ben Sedley, 2017.

WEBSITES

Because of You:
BecauseOfYou.org

Born This Way Foundation:
BornThisWay.foundation

The Center for Compassion Focused
Therapy: MindfulCompassion.com

Center for Mindful Self-Compassion:
CenterForMSC.org

Half of Us:
HalfOfUs.com

Rise Together:
WeAllRiseTogether.org

Self-Compassion: Dr. Kristin Neff:
Self-Compassion.org

Strength of Us:
StrengthOfUs.org

TeensHealth:
TeensHealth.org

The Trevor Project:
TheTrevorProject.org

Your Life Your Voice:
YourLifeYourVoice.org

APPS

Headspace: meditation app

MBLC-YA: mindfulness for teens

Real Talk: stories by teens

SuperBetter: resilience training

Teen Breathe: a well-being magazine

Teen Talk: teens supporting teens

Vent: a social diary for feelings

Wysa: mental health support

INSTAGRAM

@littlearthlings

@marcelailustra

@selfcareisforeveryone

@teentalkapp

@theofficialsadghostclub

RESOURCES FOR PARENTS

BOOKS

The Available Parent: Expert Advice for Raising Successful and Resilient Teens and Tweens by John Duffy, 2014.

The Conscious Parent: Transforming Ourselves, Empowering Our Children by Shefali Tsabary, 2010.

Ending the Parent-Teen Control Battle: Resolve the Power Struggle and Build Trust, Responsibility, and Respect by Neil D. Brown, 2016.

The Grown-Up's Guide to Teenage Humans: How to Decode Their Behavior, Develop Trust, and Raise a Respectable Adult by Josh Shipp, 2017.

Helping Your Anxious Teen: Positive Parenting Strategies to Help Your Teen Beat Anxiety, Stress, and Worry by Sheila Achar Josephs, 2016.

Parenting the New Teen in the Age of Anxiety: A Complete Guide to Your Child's Stressed, Depressed, Expanded, Amazing Adolescence by John Duffy, 2019.

Queen Bees and Wannabes, 3rd Edition: Helping Your Daughter Survive Cliques, Gossip, Boys, and the New Realities of Girl World by Rosalind Wiseman, 2016.

Self-Compassion: The Proven Power of Being Kind to Yourself by Kristin Neff, 2011.

Untangled: Guiding Teenage Girls through the Seven Transitions into Adulthood by Lisa Damour, 2016.

PODCASTS

Mighty Parenting: raising teens, parenting young adults: Stitcher.com/podcast/mighty-parenting

Parenting Teens: The Biggest Job We'll Ever Have: HydeBiggestJob.libsyn.com

Raising Teens: RaisingTeens.podbean.com

WEBSITES

Act for Youth. ActForYouth.net/adolescence/toolkit

The Center for Compassion Focused Therapy: MindfulCompassion.com

Center for Mindful Self-Compassion: CenterForMSC.org

InnerChange: InnerChange.com/resources-for-parents

Self-Compassion: Dr. Kristin Neff: Self-Compassion.org

Society for Adolescent Health and Medicine: AdolescentHealth.org/Resources/Resources-for-Adolescents-and-Parents.aspx

Teen Esteem: TeenEsteem.org

Teen Mental Health: TeenMentalHealth.org

TeensHealth: TeensHealth.org

References

Boorstein, Sylvia. *Happiness Is an Inside Job: Practicing for a Joyful Life.* New York: Ballantine Books, 2008.

Brown, Brené. *I Thought It Was Just Me (but It Isn't): Making the Journey from "What Will People Think?" to "I Am Enough."* New York: Penguin Random House, 2007.

Chödrön, Pema. *When Things Fall Apart: Heart Advice for Difficult Times.* Boulder, CO: Shambhala Publications, 1997.

Germer, Christopher K. *The Mindful Path to Self-Compassion: Freeing Yourself from Destructive Thoughts and Emotions.* New York: Guilford Press, 2009.

Goodreads. "Brené Brown > Quotes > Quotable Quote." Accessed February 13, 2020. https://www.goodreads.com/quotes /7452474-talk-to-yourself-like-you-would -to-someone-you-love.

Kabat-Zinn, Jon. *Full Catastrophe Living (Revised Edition): Using the Wisdom of Your Body and Mind to Face Stress, Pain, and Illness.* New York: Bantam Books, 2013.

Kabat-Zinn, Jon. *Wherever You Go, There You Are: Mindfulness Meditation in Everyday Life.* New York: Hachette, 2005.

Maraboli, Steve. *Life, the Truth, and Being Free.* Port Washington, NY: A Better Today Publishing, 2009.

Murakami, Haruki. *Norwegian Wood.* New York: Vintage Books, 2000.

Neff, Kristin. "The Development and Validation of a Scale to Measure Self-Compassion." *Self and Identity* 2, no. 3 (2003): 223–50. DOI.org/10.1080/15298860309027.

Neff, Kristin. *Self-Compassion: The Proven Power of Being Kind to Yourself.* New York: HarperCollins, 2011.

Neff, Kristin, and Christopher Germer. *The Mindful Self-Compassion Workbook: A Proven Way to Accept Yourself, Build Inner Strength, and Thrive.* New York: Guilford Press, 2018.

Salzberg, Sharon. *Lovingkindness: The Revolutionary Art of Happiness.* Boston: Shambhala Publications, 2002.

Stoddard, Jill A., and Niloofar Afari. *The Big Book of ACT Metaphors: A Practitioner's Guide to Experiential Exercises and Metaphors in Acceptance and Commitment Therapy.* Oakland, CA: New Harbinger Publications, 2014.

Taylor, Jill Bolte. *My Stroke of Insight: A Brain Scientist's Personal Journey.* New York: Penguin Group, 2006.

Index

Acknowledgments

I have an abundance of gratitude for many humans in my life. First, a huge thank-you to Lori and Lorraine for guiding me with editorial brilliance in my very first published work. Thank you to Jonathan for your epic mentorship, and a shout-out to all the folks at Union Square Practice for always making our workplace not feel like work. I am grateful to my sangha at the Institute of Meditation and Psychotherapy for helping me stay grounded. Endless gratitude to my courageous grandpa Boris, who brought our family to a country where I was able to fulfill so many of my dreams. Thank you to my parents for passing on to me an ambitious nature, and thank you to my brother, Dennis, who is one of the most compassionate 19-year-olds that I've ever met. I'm especially grateful to my aunt, Yuliya, for her endless warmth, understanding, and encouragement. So much gratitude to Kelley, Val, Steven, Ana, and Sydney, who are the truest of friends. Thank you to Dylan for your heart—in a way, I wrote this for you. Finally, thank you to Olivia, who blanketed me with so much love and compassion for 15 years that I had no choice but to learn how to love myself.

About the Author

Katie Krimer, MA, LCSW, is a therapist at Union Square Practice, a thriving mental wellness practice in New York City. She is also the founder of Growspace, a growth and wellness coaching platform, where she supports humans along their self-growth journey. Katie was born in Russia and immigrated to Brooklyn when she was five years old. She was fascinated by human psychology and has been working with adolescents since she was a preteen herself. Katie's greatest passions are teaching mindfulness and self-compassion practices. She hopes one day to be a part of developing a mindfulness- and self-compassion-based curriculum for elementary and middle schools. She lives in Brooklyn and loves playing the piano and traveling in her free time.

CPSIA information can be obtained
at www.ICGtesting.com
Printed in the USA
JSHW040755030520
5472JS00004B/5

9 781646 117772